AI Essentials Guide

Principles for Navigating the Next Tech Renaissance

William Hawkins

AI Essentials Guide: Principles for Navigating the Next Tech Renaissance

William Hawkins
Caledon East, ON, Canada

ISBN-13 (pbk): 979-8-8688-0910-1   ISBN-13 (electronic): 979-8-8688-0911-8
https://doi.org/10.1007/979-8-8688-0911-8

Managing Director, Apress Media LLC: Welmoed Spahr
Acquisitions Editor: Smriti Srivastava
Desk Editor: Laura Berendson
Editorial Project Manager: Kripa Joseph

Cover designed by eStudioCalamar

Cover image designed by Unsplash

Distributed to the book trade worldwide by Springer Science+Business Media New York, 1 New York Plaza, Suite 4600, New York, NY 10004-1562, USA. Phone 1-800-SPRINGER, fax (201) 348-4505, e-mail orders-ny@springer-sbm.com, or visit www.springeronline.com. Apress Media, LLC is a California LLC and the sole member (owner) is Springer Science + Business Media Finance Inc (SSBM Finance Inc). SSBM Finance Inc is a **Delaware** corporation.

For information on translations, please e-mail booktranslations@springernature.com; for reprint, paperback, or audio rights, please e-mail bookpermissions@springernature.com.

Apress titles may be purchased in bulk for academic, corporate, or promotional use. eBook versions and licenses are also available for most titles. For more information, reference our Print and eBook Bulk Sales web page at http://www.apress.com/bulk-sales.

Any source code or other supplementary material referenced by the author in this book is available to readers on GitHub. For more detailed information, please visit https://www.apress.com/gp/services/source-code.

If disposing of this product, please recycle the paper

To Mom, Dad, John, Eddie, Richard, James, and Bumpus,

Thank you for helping me up when I fall and cheering me on when I'm on top of the world. I wouldn't be the person I am today without you guys being there to help me grow and appreciate the little things in life.

To my friends and colleagues,

Thank you for all you do; whether you know it or not, you've all been instrumental in my growth as a person and as a technologist. Without the challenges we've faced together, there would be no need for this conversation, and I probably wouldn't be the one sharing the message.

To the reader, I hope you find what you're looking for; whether it's in this book or somewhere else, there is an answer to your most burning questions.

Table of Contents

About the Author

 As an AI engineer and data scientist, **William Hawkins'** career has been a testament to the transformative power of technology. Starting as an econometrician using machine learning to solve academic problems, his journey from a citizen developer to an influential AI specialist in the Microsoft community is a story of passion, perseverance, and the pursuit of excellence.

Will's professional odyssey is marked by a series of groundbreaking achievements in the realm of data and AI. From using convolutional neural networks to value online commodities to building custom Copilots across the Microsoft stack, his work stands as a paragon of innovation.

His ventures into Digital Twins, Reinforcement Learning, Microsoft Fabric, and the OneLake data model highlight his ability to transcend conventional boundaries, integrating IoT, AI, and various analytical tools to drive business transformation.

Will embodies the spirit of responsible AI engineering, underpinned by his credentials as a 5× Microsoft Certified Professional. His holistic approach to technology, emphasizing ethical application and accessibility, makes him not just an expert but a visionary leader aiming to democratize AI's evolving role in our world.

About the Technical Reviewer

 **Kapil Bansal** is a PhD scholar and Lead DevOps engineer at S&P Global Market Intelligence, India. He has more than 15 years of experience in the IT industry, having worked on Azure cloud computing (PaaS, IaaS, and SaaS), Azure Stack, DevSecOps, Kubernetes, Terraform, Office 365, SharePoint, release management, application lifecycle management (ALM), Information Technology Infrastructure Library (ITIL), and Six Sigma. He has completed the certification program in Advanced Program in Strategy for Leaders from IIM Lucknow and Cyber Security and Cyber Defense from IIT Kanpur. He has worked with companies such as IBM India Pvt Ltd, HCL Technologies, NIIT Technologies, Encore Capital Group, and Xavient Software Solutions, Noida, and has served multiple clients based in the United States, the UK, and Africa, such as T-Mobile, World Bank Group, H&M, WBMI, Encore Capital, and Bharti Airtel (India and Africa). Kapil also reviewed *Hands-On Kubernetes on Azure: Run your applications securely and at scale on the most widely adopted orchestration platform* and *Azure Networking: Practical recipes to manage network traffic in Azure, optimize performance, and secure Azure resources* published by Packt and also *Practical Microsoft Azure IaaS: Migrating and Building Scalable and Secure Cloud Solutions* and *Beginning SharePoint Communication Sites* published by Apress and many more.

Prologue

Welcome!

Imagine falling asleep in the world of 2010, a time when smartphones were just beginning their rise and "smart" was a term rarely applied to everyday objects. Now, envision waking up in today's world, where artificial intelligence silently orchestrates your morning routine—from the perfectly timed brewing of your coffee to the personalized news digest waiting on your phone. This isn't science fiction; it's the reality of how artificial intelligence (referred to as AI from here on out) and algorithms have seamlessly woven into the fabric of our daily lives, streamlining the ordinary, transforming the mundane, and reviving the human in the loop.

This is a story about that extraordinary change, told through the lens of a collection of conversations.

As human beings, we often overlook the profound role communication plays in our lives and our identity. As the only species classified as intelligent beings in this vast universe, we have an innate ability to share our thoughts, ideas, feelings, aspirations, fears, and dreams with each other. We can express almost anything in countless unique and beautiful ways. From paintings that can evoke tears to sounds that stir deep emotions and words so powerful that over 7000 different languages [1] have evolved to convey them, our capacity for communication is truly astounding. We're truly blessed to be gifted with so many forms of expression that we can tailor to our own unique experience. Moreover, we have seen these forms of expression evolve, transform, and shift millions of times over the entirety of human existence.

Most importantly, in the last 10 years, we've seen a new medium emerge that can not only understand how we express but actually create and express in very similar ways. Artificial intelligence has transformed the way humans' express ideas, knowledge, opinions, and many other key slices of the human condition by replicating and generating communication forms that have been known to only be used by humans.

Moreover, recent breakthroughs in natural language processing (NLP) and generative artificial intelligence (GAI) have launched the capabilities of this medium to levels relevant to each and every one of us.

What I want to share with you are the building blocks to using this technology to grow yourself, your business, and your life. AI has transformed not only the world around me but the world in me, and that's an experience that is worth sharing with you.

This story will take place through a series of conversations between myself and ChatGPT. The point of this approach is not to show you how to write a prompt, use a plug-in, or have ChatGPT write the book for me. It is to bring to center stage the value AI has to offer to every avenue of your life and why it is not the rocket science or mystical device from the future it has been made out to be.

For the remainder of the book, you will come across excerpts like the following:

> *Will: That's a great way of putting it. Thank you. Now, there's obviously different types of AI, can you elaborate on that a little?*
>
> *ChatGPT: Of course, Will. AI is a vast field, and not all AI systems are created equal. They vary based on their capabilities, complexities, and objectives. Let's delve into the primary classifications:*

in which I use the ChatGPT service to create a dialogue to drive the narrative forward. This is used to create a conversational structure to the content, similar to a podcast, to better disseminate the core knowledge of the book. No information used from the conversation with ChatGPT is unverified, and all supporting reference materials are available at the end of the book.

I truly hope this helps shine a light on what AI truly is and where it can provide value in your world.

Cheers, Will

CHAPTER 1

The Break of Dawn

We stand at the threshold of a revolution, where AI emerges not just as a tool, but as a catalyst reshaping every facet of our existence.

The idea of this story is to share the building blocks of AI in a way that enables you to use this technology effectively to grow yourself, your business, and your life. To be successful in this endeavor, we're going to approach these building blocks like constructing a house of understanding.

We'll start with the foundation:

1. *A VERY Light Introduction*

    We'll start by focusing on the chronology of AI development and exactly what's taken us from the Turing test to IBM's Deep Blue, to ChatGPT. We'll look at how these historical events helped shape the discipline of AI—the study of mimicking the human mind with technology and its applications today.

    We'll then detail this picture by exploring the current state of AI and discuss the essential ingredients in AI models and how changes in these ingredients have produced rapid innovation in the capabilities of models.

Finally, we'll set the tone for our journey with a short discussion on the promise of AI: what value it offers, what to be cognizant of, and how to embrace it in your world.

2. *The Basics of AI*

Here, we're going to be diving into the absolute fundamentals. There are no prerequisites; you do not have to have **any** knowledge or experience using, playing, or working with AI to understand and find relevance in this chapter.

We'll first cover what AI is, then talk about the different types (narrow/traditional vs. generative), then how it works (an overview of machine learning, deep learning, and neural networks), and close with an explanation of the learning process, i.e., how AI learns today.

Then, we'll construct our house of understanding by exploring AI's role in our spheres:

3. *AI and Personal Growth*

The most fitting beginning for discussing AI's applications seems to be where it's being felt the most: in our day-to-day.

This chapter will walk you through what using AI as a practical lifestyle choice is all about. We'll focus on how it can be used for learning and managing your time and how it can play a great role in your overall well-being, if used wisely (which we'll also discuss).

4. *AI in Business*

    As a natural next step, we'll then explore where, how, and why AI fits into the evolving business landscape.

    This will be accomplished through explaining how you can use AI as a Swiss Army knife for scaling and personalizing your business as well as its deep impact on efficiency, decision-making, and democratizing innovation.

    We'll also cover exactly what is required to be successful in using AI to grow your business. This involves exploring the implications and reliance on data, AI development systems, and how to be an AI company at the core.

5. *Using AI Responsibly*

    "With great power comes great responsibility"— Stan Lee. We put this principle into practice in this section by identifying where the bright promise of AI meets the intricate and significant challenges of moral choices.

    This will be done by traveling through other's AI failures and extracting the learnings from their mistakes. We'll also discuss principles for guiding responsible AI innovation and how to understand and manage AI-induced job displacement.

6. *The Fundamentals of AI Governance*

   Knowing how to use AI is not just about prompting or checking for hallucinations. In this chapter, we'll examine exactly what methodologies, design frameworks, and best practices produce safe, secure, reliable, and impactful AI systems at any scale.

7. *Equipping You for the AI Horizon*

   This chapter will help you see how to cultivate the essential skills, harness the power of community, and turn the challenge of an AI-driven future into your greatest adventure.

   We'll explore things like foundational skills, adaptable learning strategies, finding trusted sources, and how to get involved in the right communities for you.

Finally, we'll finish things off with some closing thoughts to take into the next chapter of your AI learning journey.

And, with us on this exploration will be our conversational collaborator, ChatGPT:

Will: Are you ready to start, and would you like me to give you a pen name in the book?

OpenAI's ChatGPT: If you'd like to give me a pen name, that could be a fun and engaging way to present the content to your readers. What name did you have in mind?

Will: What about Machine Intelligence Response Author (M.I.R.A)?

Mira: Good choice! Let's dive in.

CHAPTER 2

Glimpses of a Digital Mind

While AI may be new to you, it's an area of study that has been quietly shaping our world since the dawn of time.

And by the dawn of time, I mean the 1950s, of course.

A common misconception in the information technology (IT) industry is that AI is new technology. That recent breakthroughs are the start of its practicality and accessibility in day-to-day activities.

Though it is true that the latest decade has seen the most prominent breakthroughs in AI development and application, this is not a flash in the pan. It is more of a coronation following decades of intense research and experimentation.

If we think about when computers began to become a prominent part of our lives (this doesn't apply to you born with a computer in your hand), this too was simply an accumulation of milestones in the progress of converting the concept or idea of a personal device into a tangible, usable, and affordable household item.

In fact, the first computer was invented by Charles Babbage (1822) but was not built until 1991 [1]!

Why mention this? I'm a firm believer that incremental and consistent effort is the greatest predictor of viable, meaningful, and sustainable progress, and there is reliability in that.

W. Hawkins, *AI Essentials Guide*, https://doi.org/10.1007/979-8-8688-0911-8_2

So, for those worried that AI may simply be a fad that's gone viral, let's explore a short timeline of what has got us to today in order to illuminate why that is not the case.

Will: From my knowledge, AI really started around the 1950s and 1960s and was first experimented with during the Turing tests. Is that accurate?

Mira: Yes, your statement is broadly accurate, but let's provide a bit more nuance:

1. *The 1950s and 1960s are often considered the birth of modern AI. During this period, the field of AI research was officially founded and started to take shape.*

2. *In 1950, Alan Turing introduced the Turing test in his seminal paper "Computing Machinery and Intelligence." The Turing test was proposed as a measure of a machine's ability to exhibit intelligent behavior indistinguishable from that of a human.*

3. *In 1956, the Dartmouth Workshop took place. John McCarthy, who is one of the attendees, coined the term "artificial intelligence." This workshop is widely recognized as the birthplace of AI as a discipline.*

Note   According to Harvard historical papers, the "Computing Machinery and Intelligence" paper was where Turing discussed how to build intelligent machines and how to test their intelligence [2]. This is some needed context for our exploration of AI throughout this book. Alan Turing and John McCarthy, AI's ancestors, started the framework for critically thinking about intelligent machines and artificial intelligence as an area of research and development.

This is a prerequisite for most of the topics we will be discussing because I want you to see through your own eyes the exact nature of where AI's capabilities end and where humans are still needed in a more refined capacity.

> *Mira: After initial excitement and some progress in the late 1950s and 1960s, the field encountered several technical limitations and faced periods of reduced funding and interest, known as "AI winters."*

This is the truth that has plagued AI right from its initial inception. At a fundamental level, AI models rely on two resources to operate: data and computing power. We will revisit some of the intricacies of these two elements throughout the book but here's their roles at a base level:

Data: AI models need data because it is what they use to complete a task. It's where "intelligence" actually comes from. Imagine you went five days without any sleep or food, how great do you think your ability to function would be? That is the equivalent of an AI model without data. It cannot do anything. This is because AI models rely on data to identify and recognize patterns (learn) in order to generate/predict new values (complete tasks). This is what we see with tools like ChatGPT or DALL-E. They are essentially huge data processors that use the information at their disposal to make guesses as to what comes next in the pattern.

Computing Power: More commonly referred to as "compute," this controls an AI model's performance. In your case, think about not having access to transportation, the Internet, and shelter/living space. An AI model without compute does not have the resources to train, predict, or interact with anything in any way. It's essentially stuck just like we would be if we didn't have those vital resources.

> *Will: Can you describe to the reader some of the computational and data limitations that plagued the growth of AI from the 1960s to the present?*

Mira: As the adage goes, "Rome wasn't built in a day." In similar vein, the AI landscape we see today has undergone several transformations, each impeded by its own unique challenges.

From the 1960s to the present, computational limitations have been at the forefront of these impediments. Let's delve into some of the most prominent:

1. Insufficient Processing Power

The ambitions of early AI pioneers often outpaced the hardware available. The computational power of machines in the 1960s and 1970s was a far cry from what we have today. For instance, the operations that modern deep learning models execute in seconds could have taken months or even years back then!

Additionally, while we have made astronomical progress in computational power, large-scale models today, like GPT-4 or even more extensive iterations, still require supercomputing capabilities, highlighting the perpetual need for more processing power.

2. Limited Memory and Storage

Storage was expensive and limited. This constraint made it challenging to build and train larger models, store vast datasets, or even run experiments for extended periods. Though storage is no longer as significant a limitation, managing memory efficiently remains a challenge, especially when training large models or handling real-time data streams.

3. Lack of Large and Diverse Datasets

Data is the fuel for many AI models, especially those based on machine learning. In the initial years, there was a dearth of structured, high-quality data, limiting the potential of data-driven approaches. Today, while we're in the age of big data, the challenge has shifted to curating unbiased, representative datasets and ensuring data privacy and ethics.

What's important to note here is that there were actually two technological revolutions that were prerequisites for the current AI one we're experiencing.

1. Both insufficient processing power and limited storage were solved or greatly mitigated by the cloud infrastructure revolution which moved organizations away from physical servers that faced physical limitations.

2. As Mira mentioned, the big data revolution has greatly improved the availability of large, quality datasets for AI to be trained on, which is built on the back of the Internet revolution; the great Eric Schmidt, ex-Executive Chairman at Google, once said:

There were 5 exabytes of information created between the dawn of civilization and 2003. Now, that much information is created every two days.

And there was of course the effect of economies of scale. According to Rockwell Anyoha from the Harvard blog:

Before 1949 computers lacked a key prerequisite for intelligence: they couldn't store commands, only execute them. In other words, computers could be told what to do but couldn't remember what they did. Second, computing was extremely expensive. In the early 1950s, the cost of leasing a computer ran up to $200,000 a month. Only prestigious universities and big technology companies could afford to dillydally in these uncharted waters. A proof of concept as well as advocacy from high profile people were needed to persuade funding sources that machine intelligence was worth pursuing. [3]

9

Taking these feats into consideration, it's easy to see that the current AI revolution is more of an amalgamation of milestones rather than a magical breakthrough in modern technology. For the last 70 years, we've been preparing for AI by growing our computing and data capabilities and finding ways to make them economical at the same time!

Will: So, why now, has AI become such a hot topic? Other than the release of you, the GPT-4 model.

Mira: The resurgence and prominence of AI in recent years can be attributed to a confluence of factors, not just the release of models like GPT-4. The roots of today's AI excitement can be traced back to multiple interconnected developments:

1. *Explosion of Data: In the era of social media, smartphones, IoT devices, and more, we're generating data at an unprecedented rate. This abundance of data provides the necessary fuel for training sophisticated AI models.*

2. *Advancements in Hardware: The advent of graphics processing units (GPUs) and tensor processing units (TPUs) has dramatically accelerated AI computations. These specialized chips are adept at handling the parallel processing requirements of large neural networks.*

3. *Breakthroughs in Algorithms: While neural networks have been around since the 1960s, they faced numerous challenges. Breakthroughs like the introduction of ReLU (rectified linear units) activations, better optimization techniques (like Adam optimizer), and architectures like convolutional neural networks (CNNs) and transformers have revamped their potential.*

4. *Achievements in Deep Learning: The success of deep learning in tasks like image recognition (e.g., ImageNet competition) and natural language processing (NLP) showcased its potential and invigorated the field.*

5. *Open Source Movement: Large organizations like Google, Facebook, and OpenAI have been releasing their tools, libraries (like TensorFlow and PyTorch), and sometimes even models to the public. This democratization allows a broad community of developers and researchers to experiment, innovate, and implement AI.*

6. *Economic Opportunities: Businesses see the vast potential for AI to increase efficiency, reduce costs, generate new revenue streams, and create competitive advantages. This business interest drives investment and research.*

7. *General Public Interest: As AI technologies have found their way into consumer products—from voice assistants like Alexa to recommendation systems on platforms like Netflix—the general public has become more aware and intrigued by its potential.*

8. *Shift in Research Paradigms: Earlier, AI research was more siloed. The current trend encourages interdisciplinary approaches, merging insights from neuroscience, cognitive science, statistics, and computer science.*

9. *Global Collaboration: The Internet and online platforms have enabled AI researchers across the world to collaborate, share findings, and build upon each other's work rapidly.*

10. *Prominent Success Stories: Milestones like AlphaGo defeating world champion Go players or breakthroughs in medical AI for diagnostics have caught media attention, underscoring AI's potential.*

While the release of models like GPT-4 grabs headlines, they are just the tip of the iceberg. The current AI renaissance is a culmination of decades of perseverance, innovation, and a series of fortuitous events aligning in the field's favor.

Couldn't have put it better myself; we are living through the most recent technology renaissance. The 1920s had the radio, the 1960s had spaceships, the 1980s had the Internet, and today, we have AI.

Outside of the economic lenses for why AI is important now, there are the social considerations that have helped drive the pace of innovation equivalently, if not more so.

Will: Mira, why has society evolved to embrace AI?

Mira: Society's evolution to embrace AI can be attributed to several interconnected factors that span technological advancements, economic incentives, cultural shifts, and practical benefits. Here's a closer look at why society has increasingly accepted and integrated AI:

1. *Practical Benefits and Efficiency Gains*

    • *Enhanced Productivity: AI automates routine and repetitive tasks, freeing up human workers to focus on more complex and creative tasks. This leads to increased productivity and efficiency across various sectors.*

12

- *Improved Decision-Making: AI systems can analyze vast amounts of data quickly and accurately, providing insights that help individuals and organizations make better decisions.*

2. *Consumer Convenience and Personalization*

   - *Everyday Applications: AI has been integrated into everyday consumer technology, such as smartphones, smart home devices, and personal assistants like Siri and Alexa. These applications provide convenience and improve the quality of life.*

   - *Personalized Experiences: AI-driven personalization in services like recommendations on Netflix, targeted advertising, and customized news feeds enhances user experiences by catering to individual preferences.*

3. *Economic Growth and Innovation*

   - *New Markets and Opportunities: AI has opened up new markets and business opportunities, driving economic growth. Industries ranging from healthcare to finance are leveraging AI to innovate and improve their services.*

   - *Competitive Advantage: Businesses that adopt AI can gain a competitive edge by optimizing operations, reducing costs, and offering new and improved products and services.*

4. *Cultural and Social Shifts*

- *Normalization Through Media: Media and popular culture have played a role in normalizing AI. Positive portrayals of AI in movies, TV shows, and news stories have helped mitigate fears and build acceptance.*

- *Digital Natives: Younger generations, who have grown up with technology, are more comfortable and familiar with AI. This generational shift has contributed to a broader acceptance of AI technologies.*

5. *Educational and Awareness Efforts*

- *Public Education: Efforts to educate the public about AI, its capabilities, and its limitations have demystified the technology. Increased understanding leads to greater acceptance and trust.*

- *Transparency: Companies and organizations have made efforts to be transparent about how AI systems work and how they use data, building public trust.*

6. *Ethical and Responsible AI Development*

- *Ethical Guidelines: The development and implementation of ethical guidelines for AI use have addressed concerns about bias, privacy, and security. These guidelines help ensure that AI is used responsibly and fairly.*

- *AI for Social Good: Highlighting AI's potential for positive impact, such as in healthcare advancements, environmental monitoring, and disaster response, has shifted the narrative toward the beneficial uses of AI.*

7. *Government and Institutional Support*

    - *Policy and Regulation: Government policies and regulations that support AI research and development have encouraged its growth and integration into society.*

    - *Public–Private Partnerships: Collaborations between governments, academia, and the private sector have fostered innovation and the responsible deployment of AI technologies.*

8. *Adaptation and Resilience*

    - *Workforce Adaptation: The workforce has adapted to AI integration through upskilling and reskilling initiatives. Educational institutions and employers are focusing on equipping individuals with the skills needed to work alongside AI.*

    - *Resilient Economies: Economies have shown resilience by adapting to technological changes and leveraging AI to address new challenges and opportunities.*

In summary, society's embrace of AI is driven by a combination of practical benefits, economic incentives, cultural normalization, educational efforts, ethical considerations, and institutional support. These factors collectively contribute to the acceptance and integration of AI as a valuable tool in enhancing various aspects of life.

I've often found myself in discussion with my parents or colleagues about how the gadgets showcased in *Star Trek* really inspired the majority of the most prominent innovations of the last couple of decades. The smartphone, 3D printer, web conferencing, and universal translation software are just a handful of devices once imagined transformed into real inventions [4].

AI is no different; whether it's *Star Wars*, *Terminator*, or *I, Robot*, there has been an abundance of depictions of robots and other intelligent machines that, even though created for a fictional purpose, provided real value (when shown in a positive light).

For example, C-3P0 from *Star Wars* is fluent in over 6 million forms of communication which is a bit more than the number of languages spoken on Earth, but an assistant, software, or application that is capable of this ability is incredibly valuable for Earth people too!

This is an essential aspect of what's allowed AI to flourish in the most recent decade; with this conceptual understanding of what benefits AI could provide, society has been able to find an easier path to accepting the technology as embraceable in modern day.

The other keystone that's resulted in a greater social acceptance of AI is the growing necessity for intelligent tools. Satya Nadella, current CEO of Microsoft, put it best:

> *AI can help you act more effectively without needing to speak computer.*

In reality, this is the biggest reason for AI becoming a hot topic. The latest innovations are the first milestone of a human being able to instruct a computer on what to do in their natural language and the machine actually understands what they are saying.

This is much more of an "inspiration from desperation" kind of commodity; as the digital world continues to synthesize more and more with our physical world, having tools that can not only speak our native tongue but actually understand context, nuance, and, in essence, what the heck you're trying to do on the computer is critical.

A survey of knowledge workers across 300 enterprises by 1E found that 95% of employees say they "struggle with digital friction such as software and network issues, workplace application access problems, and slow devices" [5].

We've all encountered this struggle; you fire up your computer to complete what should be a simple task and end up fighting with Google, some software, or another part of your machine for half the day. And, up until 2022, you couldn't just open up ChatGPT or Microsoft Copilot and say exactly what you wanted and how you wanted it.

Finally, there is the data science aspect of it all.

Will: Mira, what is data science? It kind of seems like a bit of operations research and statistics.

Mira: Great question! Data science indeed overlaps with fields like operations research and statistics, but it has its own unique characteristics and applications. Let's break it down.

Data science is an interdisciplinary field that uses scientific methods, processes, algorithms, and systems to extract knowledge and insights from structured and unstructured data. It involves a combination of skills from various domains, including statistics, computer science, domain expertise, and mathematics, to analyze and interpret complex data.

Key Components of Data Science

1. *Data Collection*

    -   *Gathering data from various sources, such as databases, web scraping, sensors, and more.*

    -   *Ensuring data quality and completeness.*

2. *Data Cleaning and Preparation*

    - *Cleaning data to remove errors, inconsistencies, and missing values.*

    - *Transforming and formatting data to make it suitable for analysis.*

3. *Exploratory Data Analysis (EDA)*

    - *Using statistical methods and visualization tools to understand the data's underlying patterns, distributions, and relationships.*

    - *Identifying key variables and trends.*

4. *Statistical Analysis and Modeling*

    - *Applying statistical techniques to analyze data and test hypotheses.*

    - *Building predictive models using machine learning algorithms to forecast future trends or behaviors.*

5. *Machine Learning and Algorithms*

    - *Implementing machine learning algorithms to build models that can learn from data and make predictions or classifications.*

    - *Techniques include regression, classification, clustering, and neural networks.*

6. *Data Visualization*

    - *Creating visual representations of data to communicate findings effectively.*

    - *Tools like Matplotlib, Seaborn, Tableau, and Power BI are commonly used.*

7. *Data Interpretation and Insights*

    - *Interpreting the results of data analysis and modeling to derive actionable insights.*

    - *Communicating these insights to stakeholders through reports, dashboards, and presentations.*

8. *Deployment and Monitoring*

    - *Deploying data science models into production environments where they can be used for real-time decision-making.*

    - *Monitoring and maintaining models to ensure they continue to perform well over time.*

How Data Science Relates to Other Fields

1. *Statistics: Statistics provides the foundational techniques for data analysis, such as hypothesis testing, regression, and probability theory. Data science builds on these techniques and integrates them with computational methods.*

2. *Operations Research: Operations research focuses on optimizing complex systems and decision-making processes using mathematical modeling, statistical analysis, and optimization techniques. Data science often uses similar methods for data analysis and modeling but is broader in scope, encompassing machine learning, big data, and more.*

3. *Computer Science: Data science heavily relies on computer science for data processing, algorithm development, and programming. It involves writing code, managing databases, and using software tools to analyze and visualize data.*

19

Applications of Data Science

1.   *Business: Data science is used for customer segmentation, market analysis, fraud detection, and recommendation systems.*

2.   *Healthcare: Applications include predictive analytics for patient outcomes, medical imaging analysis, and personalized medicine.*

3.   *Finance: Risk management, algorithmic trading, credit scoring, and customer analytics are common use cases.*

4.   *Technology: Search engines, speech recognition, image classification, and autonomous systems are driven by data science.*

5.   *Social Sciences: Analyzing social media trends, public opinion, and demographic studies.*

In summary, data science is a multidisciplinary field that blends statistics, computer science, and domain expertise to analyze data and extract meaningful insights. Its applications are vast and diverse, making it a powerful tool in today's data-driven world.

The reason I wanted to bring an overview of what data science is into this discussion is to highlight exactly what's been bringing this perfect storm of innovation to life.

Like many of the other phenomena I've described up to this point, data science is not really nascent.

The roots of data science can be traced back to the 1960s and 1970s when computer science and statistics began to intersect. During this time, statisticians were among the first to realize the potential of computers for data analysis [6].

This is what lies at the heart of modern AI. It is taking the data points available for a specific behavior you're trying to understand in the world (e.g., why salmon swim upstream or why people buy fast food) and creating a conceptual model of the cause-and-effect variables that influence that behavior.

In layman's terms, it's using data to create an understanding of how something works.

What the field of data science has done is pair this modelling with whatever technology is available to create something "intelligent."

For anyone brand spanking new to this discipline, this is the root of what's called machine learning, or ML for short. You are creating artificial intelligence by creating a model of data points using a machine (usually referred to as an algorithm); hence, the machine **learns** the behavior (more on this in the next chapter).

So, at the end of the day, data science is the catalyst for taking all of the innovations of cloud computing, big data, the Internet, and creating AI solutions (robots, software, etc.) that address economic and social challenges with data-driven capabilities.

But, how has all of this made AI relevant to your day-to-day activities?

The advent of ChatGPT (or, in the guise of this book, Mira) has sparked the rise of democratizing the use of AI for day-to-day activities. The fact that an AI model is at your fingertips anytime, anywhere with ChatGPT or Microsoft Copilot is a major indicator of it being more than just hype. You don't have to be a mathematician to engineer a prompt, and you don't need an abundance of computer power to use a model for simple questions and tasks. That is significant, real-world, value.

Will: Thank you, Mira, that is well said. Now, we'll of course highlight what AI can't do and the limitations of what we have access to today later, but to close out the chapter, can you briefly describe exactly what AI can do for the reader today?

Mira: Absolutely, Will. It's crucial for readers to have a balanced understanding of AI's capabilities. So, while AI is not a silver bullet, its current applications are both broad and impactful. In essence, AI is becoming a silent partner in many aspects of our daily lives, amplifying human capabilities, automating routine tasks, and providing insights that were previously out of reach. As technology evolves, the potential applications will only expand, making it an exciting era for anyone eager to find the value in AI.

Summary: Glimpses of a Digital Mind

Historical Context and Misconceptions

Artificial intelligence (AI) may seem like a modern phenomenon, but its roots trace back to the 1950s. Despite recent breakthroughs making AI practical and accessible, the field's development has been a gradual process built on decades of research and experimentation. Early computing milestones laid the groundwork, with Charles Babbage conceptualizing the first computer in 1822, though it wasn't built until 1991.

Early Developments in AI

AI research began to take shape in the 1950s and 1960s, with key events including

- *1950:* Alan Turing introduced the Turing test to measure machine intelligence.

- *1956:* John McCarthy coined the term "artificial intelligence" at the Dartmouth Workshop, marking the birth of AI as a discipline.

Challenges and AI Winters

The journey of AI has been marked by periods of high expectations followed by "AI winters," times of reduced funding, and interest due to technical limitations:

- *Data and Computing Power:* AI models require vast amounts of data and significant computing power to function effectively. Early computers lacked the processing power and memory to support advanced AI, and large datasets were scarce.

Technological Revolutions Enabling AI

Several technological advancements have paved the way for the current AI revolution:

- *Cloud Computing:* Mitigated limitations in storage and processing power

- *Big Data:* Provided the vast amounts of data necessary for training AI models

- *Economies of Scale:* Made technology more affordable and accessible

Recent Advances and Factors Driving AI

AI's resurgence is driven by multiple factors:

- *Explosion of Data:* The digital age has led to unprecedented data generation.

- *Advancements in Hardware:* GPUs and TPUs have accelerated AI computations.

- *Algorithmic Breakthroughs:* Innovations like CNNs and transformers have enhanced AI capabilities.

- *Achievements in Deep Learning:* Success in fields like image recognition and NLP.

- *Open Source Movement:* Tools and libraries made available by organizations.

- *Economic Opportunities:* AI offers significant business advantages.

- *Public Interest:* AI in consumer products has increased awareness and acceptance.

- *Interdisciplinary Research:* Collaboration across various fields has fueled innovation.

- *Global Collaboration:* The Internet has enabled rapid sharing and building upon research.

- *Prominent Success Stories:* High-profile AI achievements have captured public imagination.

Societal Acceptance of AI

Society has embraced AI due to its practical benefits and efficiency gains. AI enhances productivity, improves decision-making, and offers personalized consumer experiences. Economic growth and new business opportunities further drive AI integration. Cultural shifts, media normalization, and education efforts have demystified AI, while ethical guidelines and responsible development build trust.

Data Science and AI

Data science, an interdisciplinary field combining statistics, computer science, and domain expertise, plays a crucial role in AI development. It involves

- *Data Collection and Cleaning:* Ensuring high-quality data

- *Exploratory Data Analysis:* Understanding data patterns

- *Statistical Analysis and Modeling:* Building predictive models

- *Machine Learning:* Implementing algorithms for predictions

- *Data Visualization:* Communicating insights effectively

- *Deployment and Monitoring:* Maintaining model performance in real-world applications

The Democratization of AI

Tools like ChatGPT have democratized AI, making it accessible for everyday use. AI can now assist with a wide range of tasks without requiring specialized knowledge or resources.

Current Capabilities of AI

Today, AI amplifies human capabilities, automates routine tasks, and provides valuable insights across various domains. While not a panacea, AI's applications are extensive and continue to expand, offering significant real-world value and potential for future growth.

CHAPTER 3

Illuminating the Enigma: Deciphering the Basics of AI

When I say "deciphering the basics," I mean we're going to carefully walk through and build the fundamental understanding of what artificial intelligence is and how, at a fundamental level, it works.

It's important to note that there is absolutely **no** prerequisite knowledge required to understand this chapter. I've designed it specifically to be as easy to digest as possible regardless of any previous experience or lack of that you have with AI.

The reason for this approach and particularly what I want you to focus on when reading is to mitigate confusion. There are a lot of complex intricacies in AI jargon and data science research that make academic publications a stretch to read. Trust me, I struggle digesting that content as much as the next person.

This confusion easily causes misconstrued beliefs, and that is in large part one of the main obstacles when it comes to increasing data and AI literacy. How can you embrace something that you don't understand?

Moreover, how can you properly embrace AI if you're afraid of it? And I don't just mean it becoming a Terminator but real risks like it breaching sensitive data or impersonating someone.

There is a mountain of AI content out there in the big wide world, and it seems like an even 50/50 split of good and bad. Some will be helpful; some will be harmful, and I'm hoping that this chapter and this book in general doesn't just add to the positive column but actually corrects limiting beliefs or relieves confusion from the firehose that is the Internet.

By the end of this chapter, you will have the ability to unravel the mystery of how machines mimic the marvels of the human mind.

Arthur C. Clarke once said:

> *Any sufficiently advanced technology is indistinguishable from magic.*

Right now, this probably feels like the most relatable thing about AI. All these fancy terms—LLMs, GPTs, CNNs, ReLUs—seem cool at first but get very scary, very quick.

Don't worry! There is no test or homework on these terms; I'll make sure they are well explained (in layman's terms).

Moreover, I have a story that should help set the tone. In my first ever "real job," I was a data analyst for a division of the government that produced statistics on a handful of economic sectors.

In the first month or so, I found myself in a meeting where a couple of data scientists were presenting some of the work they were doing on their side of the department. I was so fascinated; I messaged one of the presenters after the meeting finished and asked if I could meet with him and pick his brain.

Don't worry, there is a point coming, I promise!

The day comes for the meeting; I have all my very intuitive questions prepared, and I'm ready for the call. The questions were so intuitive that I forgot them by the time I started writing this book.

We get on the call, and I do my absolute best to not act like a super fan.

I asked him something around what the career of a data scientist looks like since that's what I was aspiring to become. His answer was approximately this:

A data scientist's job is to take very confusing, intricate, and difficult data and explain it to decision-makers. We are essentially the wizards that wave a wand that turns data into diamonds.

That's what my objective is with this chapter. No, there is no magic wand (though, that would be cool); I will be explaining in the simplest of all terms how AI works. So, put your notepad away and grab a box of popcorn...this is going to be a SHOW!

Will: Alright Mira, let's start with the basics. In super simple terms, what is artificial intelligence, better known as AI?

Mira: Great place to start, Will. At its core, artificial intelligence, or AI, is the attempt to make machines think and act like humans. It's about designing systems that can perform tasks that normally require human intelligence. This includes things like understanding language, recognizing patterns, solving problems, making decisions, and even potentially having creativity. In essence, it's teaching machines to mimic or simulate aspects of human cognition. Think of it as giving computers a bit of a "brain" to handle tasks in a more human-like way!

Mira's not far off. According to the well-known publishing platform, Medium:

The shortest definition of AI could be, Machine's that have cognitive intelligence, in short, act like humans. In simple terms, Artificial Intelligence (AI) refers to the simulation of human intelligence in machines that are programmed to think like humans and mimic their cognitive actions. It includes learning, reasoning, problem-solving, and perception. In other words, creating a machine capable of understanding the environment, understanding the problem, and acting intelligently according to the situation. Basically, machines make decisions like human beings, and at some point, outperforming them. [1]

Will: According to Medium, AI is about making machines make decisions like human beings and, at some point, outperforming them. What do you make of this?

Mira: That's a common perspective, Will. Let's break it down:

- *Making Decisions Like Humans: Yes, one of the goals of AI is to enable machines to make decisions in a manner similar to humans. This doesn't just mean processing data and following pre-set rules, but interpreting context, understanding nuances, and even learning from past experiences.*

- *Outperforming Humans: Here's where it gets intriguing. In many specific tasks, AI already outperforms humans, especially where vast amounts of data are involved. For instance, an AI can analyze thousands of medical images in minutes, something that would take a human radiologist significantly longer. Or consider games like Go and Chess, where certain AI models have bested world champions.*

However, it's essential to clarify that "outperforming" doesn't mean AI is superior in every aspect. AI might excel in computational tasks or data-driven decisions, but human beings possess creativity, emotional intelligence, contextual understanding, and a myriad of other cognitive abilities that AI can't replicate in totality.

So, while AI can outperform humans in specific, often narrow tasks, the broader landscape of intelligence, creativity, and emotional depth remains a distinctly human domain—at least for now.

Now, before you grab your pitchforks and head for the bunker, let's look at that one more time. AI can outperform humans in specific, often narrow tasks. Better put, they can do the things we are not built to do, better!

Building AIs is all about identifying the areas where we, as humans, struggle. We can't analyze 1000 images in 5 mins, we can't summarize a 300-page procedure without hours or days of reading, understanding, and, of course, Googling.

It's okay to acknowledge and accept that we as humans cannot do everything well, especially on our own. It's just not possible and doesn't make sense. Why is it important we do these tedious but important tasks at a snail's pace? Not to mention, we have these things called distractions that make even the most productive people less capable.

Moreover, what about the risks we generate by not being perfect at very specific tasks or when we are under pressure or duress?

I don't mean to scare you but listen to this...I did an AI use case presentation for a Microsoft competition in 2022 that revolved around how AI could be used in healthcare. My presentation covered the use of a Deep Reinforcement Learning (DRL) algorithm for pointing a laser at the exact location for surgical incisions during operations. While researching the content for the presentation, I came across this very scary term, wrong-site surgery. Do you know what that is? It is when a surgeon operates ON THE WRONG BODY PART. WHAT?! WHAT?! I didn't think that was possible.

Sorry for the monologue but this is important. According to the American College of Surgeons, in 2022, **_wrong-site surgery accounted for 6% of the 1,441 sentinel events_** reviewed by The Joint Commission [2].

The number may not seem significant, but can you fathom that, on average, you have a 6% chance of having the WRONG PART OF YOUR BODY operated on? My mind was blown to say the least.

That's why, whether you've embraced it, AI is here to stay. We as human beings do not have the capacity to do everything well nor should we try to. We are responsible for so much on a daily basis; wouldn't it be nice if you only had to focus on the **higher value tasks**? The ones that require a human touch like designing your company's strategic initiative to secure new business based on your 30 years of industry experience or carefully explaining the principles of morality to your children.

Could an AI do that stuff too? Sure. Could it do it better? No way!

As Mira mentioned, human beings possess creativity, emotional intelligence, contextual understanding, critical thinking, and a myriad of other cognitive abilities that AI can't replicate in totality, and that's where we should be focusing our attention, time, and energy.

Can you imagine how much more effective you'd be if you weren't encumbered by mundane activities that chew away your precious mental resources?

A Work Trend Index report [3] published by Microsoft found that users of their AI technology, Copilot, were

- 29% faster at searching, writing, and summarizing

- Were able to get caught up on a missed meeting nearly 4× faster

- 64% spent less time on email

No more sifting through a week's worth of email the night before your first day back from vacation when you should be spending quality time with your partner.

Or locking yourself in your "focus room" to pump out a blog post for a work deadline instead of creating the content you've always wanted to for your foodie YouTube channel.

I'm not saying to start adopting every AI that haphazardly makes its way to market nor am I saying give up on doing your priorities because "Will said AI will do it for me."

All I'm asking you to do is embrace the idea that having AI in the world can be a complement to your life, not a replacement. Trust me, there is a massive difference.

Ok...monologue over...let's get back to the story!

Will: That's a great way of putting it, thank you. Now, there's obviously different types of AI, can you elaborate on that a little?

Mira: Of course, Will. AI is a vast field, and not all AI systems are created equal. They vary based on their capabilities, complexities, and objectives. Let's delve into the primary classifications:

1. *Purpose*

    - *Narrow AI: Its main objective is to perform a specific, predefined task. Whether that's setting an alarm, answering a trivia question, or identifying objects in a photo, it operates within that confined domain.*

    - *Generative AI: Its primary goal is creation. It takes inspiration from existing data to produce or generate new, original content, whether that's an image, text, music, or even video.*

2. *Interaction*

    - *Narrow AI: Think of it as a specialist. Just like you'd go to a cardiologist specifically for heart-related issues and not for a broken bone, narrow AI is specialized in a particular function. Ask it something outside its realm, and it won't be able to assist.*

    - *Generative AI: Imagine it as an artist or composer. Given some inspiration or a theme, it can create something new based on patterns it has learned. But its output is creative rather than functional.*

3. *Example*

    - *Narrow AI: A calculator app on your phone designed to do math operations.*

    - *Generative AI: An app that can compose new melodies based on a few tunes you feed into it.*

So, in a nutshell, if an AI is performing a specific, predefined task, it's a narrow AI. If its producing new content inspired by existing data, it's a generative AI. Think of it as the difference between a specialist doctor and a musician: one has a very specific expertise, and the other creates based on inspiration!

I wanted to highlight this difference because I've encountered lots of scenarios where people struggle to really see what value AI brings to their situation. Not everybody needs a chatbot or an image generation tool, and that's totally cool! However, I do believe there is an AI for everyone and, more importantly, for almost every problem.

That being said, there are enough types of AI to fill a library so I've boiled down "the usual suspects" that should be a part of your repertoire of potential solution candidates next time you're considering using AI to solve a problem:

1. NN (Neural Network)

   What is it: A neural network is a digital brain made up of many tiny interconnected "neurons" referred to as a network. An example architecture diagram is shown in Figure 3-1.

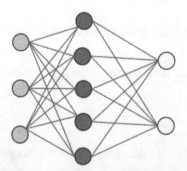

Figure 3-1. *A simple neural network, the green dots represent inputs (text, numbers, etc.), and the purple dots are a series of computations applied to the inputs so the AI can guess what the output should be. The yellow dots represent those outputs (scores, words, etc.)*

How does it work: Neural networks use data to iteratively learn how to complete a task. Just like a child learning to recognize animals, this digital brain starts out not knowing much. At first, it might get confused between a cat and a dog. But over time, with enough examples and corrections ("This is a cat, not a dog"), the neural network adjusts its internal connections and gets better at distinguishing them. A neural network learns from data the same way our brains learn from experience.

Think of a neural network as a **very** advanced relay team. Each layer of the network receives the input from the previous layer and performs some operation on the input to turn it into an output.

How you set up the network determines:

- What the AI is looking to output (a classification, a score, etc.)

- How it processes the input (types of layers)

- How long it takes to process the input (number of layers)

When to use: Neural networks are often the underlying AI architecture for an algorithm, so they are used fairly generically. Practically, any task or dataset with complexities, nuances, or large volumes will be a good fit for a neural network.

2.   CNN (Convolutional Neural Network)

What is it: A convolutional neural network is like a detective specializing in pictures. Imagine trying to recognize a face in a large painting. The process of recognizing an animal using a CNN is shown in Figure 3-2.

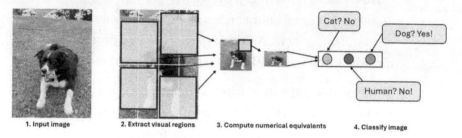

Figure 3-2. *A simple image classification CNN receiving an input image and breaking it down into a classification*

How does it work: Instead of looking at the entire painting all at once, the detective looks closely at small parts, such as the eyes, nose, and mouth. After understanding these parts, the detective pieces them together to recognize the whole face. In a similar way, a CNN takes an image, breaks it down into smaller patches, identifies patterns in these patches, and then combines these patterns to understand the entire image.

When to use: Classifying things in an image, detecting objects in an image, recognizing things in an image (e.g., Pepsi logo). Practically anything that involves image or video data will require a CNN of some kind. I once trained one to classify the quality level and size of a strawberry!

3. DNN (Deep Neural Network)

    What is it: A deep neural network (DNN) is like an upgraded version of a basic neural network. When we say "deep," we're talking about the complexity and size of the network. Think of it this way: all DNNs are neural networks, but not all neural networks have the depth to be called 'deep.' A side-by-side comparison of a simple and deep neural network architecture is shown in Figure 3-3.

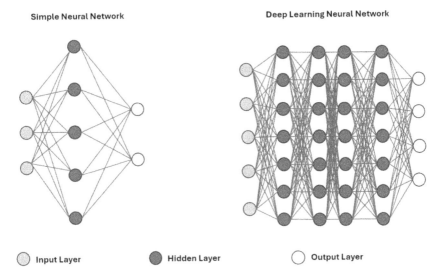

Simple Neural Network   **Deep Learning Neural Network**

◐ Input Layer   ● Hidden Layer   ○ Output Layer

Figure 3-3. *A side-by-side comparison of a regular neural network and a deep neural network. Hidden layers can be interpreted as a series of computations applied to the input data*

How does it work: To picture this, imagine roads. A basic neural network is like a small road connecting two towns. A DNN, on the other hand, is like a vast highway system linking many cities, able to handle much more traffic and navigate complex paths.

When to use it: Basically, for anything that can't be handled by a regular neural network which would usually be even larger and even more complex data (the scary stuff).

4. GPT (Generative Pre-trained Transformer)

    What is it: Imagine a student who has read and memorized countless books, articles, and papers. When you ask this student a question or to write an essay, they draw from what they've learned to answer or write. A GPT is similar. It's a type of neural network that has been trained on vast amounts of text. An example GPT architecture is shown in Figure 3-4.

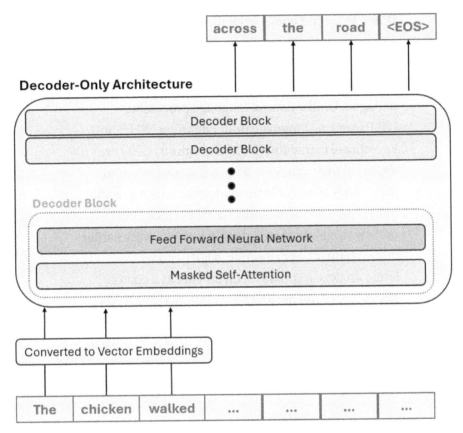

Figure 3-4. *A simple GPT architecture. The sentence at the bottom is the user input, the token and positional embedding represents the words being converted to numbers for processing. The middle block represents the NN performing computations to create new words. The top sentence is the model output. EOS stands for end of sentence*

How does it work: With this pre-memorized knowledge, it can generate new content, answer questions, or even translate languages. The "transformer" in its name refers to its advanced architecture that allows it to understand and work with text exceptionally well.

When to use it: I could write three more books on use cases exclusively for GPTs, but if I had to summarize all of them into one sentence, it would be any activity that involves intelligently processing dialogue. Unlike natural language processing (NLP), natural language understanding (NLU) and key-phrase extraction (KPE) algorithms, GPTs are designed to produce an output (like text or code) that is widely useful instead of producing a specific output relevant to a handful of tasks (recall our narrow vs. generative AI discussion with Mira earlier in the chapter). For example, a GPT can write a letter, analyze a spreadsheet, and act as a chatbot where any of the narrow AIs mentioned (NLP, NLU, and KPE) can only do a handful of sub-activities like translate a sentence of the letter from English to French, identify names in the spreadsheet, or know whether a customer is asking for a bagel or a donut.

5. LLM (Large Language Model)

What is it: Imagine a vast library filled with millions of books. Now, imagine if you had a superhuman librarian who had read all those books and could write, answer questions, or have conversations based on everything they read. An LLM is like this librarian. It's a type of neural network trained on vast amounts of text.

How it works: This allows it to understand and generate language, helping it to chat, write, or even create content as if it has consumed all those books. A GPT is a type of LLM.

When to use it: If GPTs are students and LLMs are superlibrarians, you can think of turning to LLMs when a GPT is missing the knowledge that you need. More specifically, GPTs excel in chat interactions, but a different LLM may be better suited for something not chat-based like creating an entire e-commerce website.

6. RAG (Retrieval Augmented Generation):

    What is it: Think of RAG as a student with an open-book exam. A comparison of a RAG vs non-RAG LLM workflow is shown in Figure 3-5.

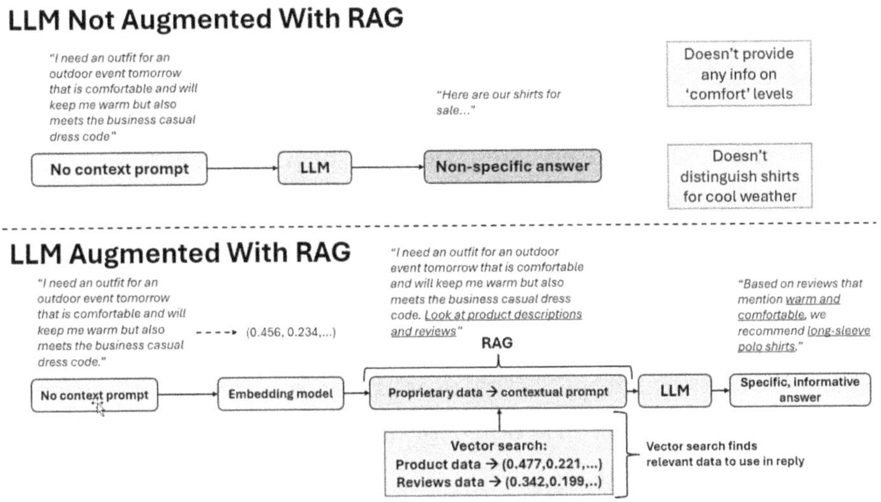

LLM Not Augmented With RAG

"I need an outfit for an outdoor event tomorrow that is comfortable and will keep me warm but also meets the business casual dress code"

"Here are our shirts for sale..."

Doesn't provide any info on 'comfort' levels

No context prompt → LLM → Non-specific answer

Doesn't distinguish shirts for cool weather

LLM Augmented With RAG

"I need an outfit for an outdoor event tomorrow that is comfortable and will keep me warm but also meets the business casual dress code."

(0.456, 0.234,...)

"I need an outfit for an outdoor event tomorrow that is comfortable and will keep me warm but also meets the business casual dress code. *Look at product descriptions and reviews*"

RAG

"Based on reviews that mention *warm and comfortable*, we recommend *long-sleeve polo shirts*."

No context prompt → Embedding model → Proprietary data → contextual prompt → LLM → Specific, informative answer

Vector search:
Product data → (0.477,0.221,...)
Reviews data → (0.342,0.199,..)

Vector search finds relevant data to use in reply

Figure 3-5. *A side-by-side comparison of using an LLM with and without RAG. "No context prompt" is the user message; the embedding model is converting this text into numbers so the LLM can read it. The RAG component is calling a vector search (searching for proprietary data in a database that is most relevant to the user message) and returning the most relevant data for the LLM to use in its answer to the user's message*

How it works: Instead of relying solely on what they've memorized, the student can fetch information from their textbook to answer questions. Similarly, RAG is an AI approach where, instead of just generating an answer from what it's memorized, the system retrieves relevant data or information first and then uses a GPT or LLM to craft a response based on that data.

When to use it: If we continue to think of GPTs or LLMs as knowledge memorizers, then the reason you would use RAG is when they would not have the knowledge you need memorized. This will most likely be information not on the Internet or publicly accessible, for example, your company code of conduct or your latest diary entry. RAG is the approach used when you want the AI to answer using your information but don't want the model to have it memorized.

Remember, this is a shortlist; there are many other types of AI that may fit better with other situations. In fact, there's enough of them to make a website about it: visit `https://theresanaiforthat.com/` so you can see exactly what's out there! I'm serious; this is a real tool that will help you find the AI or AIs for you.

It's also important to note that many of the different types of AI are simply spin-offs, variants, or advancements of other, previously existing AI types. You can see that above, DNNs are just more elaborate NNs, CNNs are just NNs focused on images, GPTs are dialogue-specialized LLMs, and RAG relies on LLMs to produce its output.

Moreover, LLMs are advanced NNs so if you can understand the principles of these usual suspects, almost any other AI you encounter will abide by these same parent-types.

Will: Ok, now that we know enough about the whole AI concept. Let's go over how they work. Remember, there is no technical expertise required to read this book so can you explain how AI works in layman's terms?

Mira: Absolutely, Will! Let's use some everyday analogies to break down how AI, particularly the underlying mechanism of machine learning (ML), works:

Imagine AI As Cooking

1. *Ingredients (Data)*

   - *Just as you need ingredients to cook a meal, AI needs data to "cook up" its knowledge. The better the ingredients, the better the dish. Similarly, the better (or more accurate) the data, the better AI can perform.*

2. *Recipe (Algorithm)*

   - *When cooking, you follow a recipe. In AI, this recipe is called an algorithm. It's a set of instructions that tells the AI how to process the data.*

3. *Taste Testing (Training)*

   - *As you cook, you might taste the dish and adjust the seasoning. In the AI world, this is training. AI uses its algorithm to "taste test" or process the data, learns from any mistakes it makes, and adjusts accordingly.*

4. *Serving the Dish (Prediction)*

   - *Once you're satisfied with the taste, you serve the dish. Similarly, once trained, the AI can now "serve" or make predictions on new data it hasn't seen before.*

5. *Feedback (Testing and Validation)*

   - *After eating, someone might give you feedback on the dish. AI has a similar phase where its predictions are tested against real outcomes to see how well it did. This feedback loop helps improve the recipe for next time.*

6. *Perfecting the Recipe (Optimization)*

   - *The more you cook and get feedback, the better your dishes become. Similarly, AI continuously learns and tweaks its algorithm to get better at its predictions.*

In summary, AI, especially machine learning, is a lot like cooking: you need the right ingredients (data), a good recipe (algorithm), taste testing (training), and feedback (testing) to perfect your dish. And just like there are different cooking techniques for various dishes, there are different AI models and algorithms for different tasks. It's all about getting the blend right!

I love this analogy. It really helps convey the whole idea of data science. Each dataset is unique in almost every way, different number of rows, columns, relationships, structure, no structure, system, data types, etc.

Most of the data collectors of the world, whether it's your local bakery, that stupid survey you took to get free credits, or Google, collect, store, and move all of that data in completely different ways. Sometimes in ways they don't even know!

That's the job of a data scientist, take the information circling the problem and use it to create a solution. Or, more specifically, an AI that solves the problem. In my opinion, building the right AI is no different than backpacking.

You've got your supplies: code, application programming interfaces (APIs), etc., your person and the world at your fingertips. Then, it comes down to charting a path and following the stars to your destination.

Ok, that was even wishy-washy for me. The point is, AI is not magic. It works in a similar fashion to most other things. You give it access to the information it needs to solve a problem, and it finds a way to get the job done, simple as that!

I hope that sheds some light on the more technical side of AI functionality. You can always email me (`will.hawkins@ritewai.com`) any questions you may have about this concept, how you implement it, or literally anything else. I am not a master, and I learn lots from the brilliant people I'm lucky to be surrounded by so the more discussions we have about the technology, the better understanding we all shall have!

With all that being said, I'm sure some of these different AI types or components may have gone over your head, and that's completely okay! Like I said, no quiz, no homework. You can do your own research if you'd like, but if the most you learned was what GPT stands for, I've done my job.

And you're in luck, throughout the next two chapters, we are going to explore how these things like neural networks are actually leveraged to make AI applicable to our day-to-day lives.

Summary: Illuminating the Enigma
Understanding AI Fundamentals

This chapter aims to demystify artificial intelligence (AI) by breaking down its fundamental concepts in an easy-to-understand manner, without requiring any prior knowledge. The objective is to clarify the complexities of AI and dispel common fears, making the subject approachable and relatable.

What Is AI?

At its core, AI is about making machines think and act like humans. It involves creating systems that can perform tasks requiring human intelligence, such as understanding language, recognizing patterns, solving problems, and making decisions. Essentially, AI gives computers the ability to mimic human cognition.

Key Concepts and Terminology

- *Artificial Intelligence (AI):* Machines designed to perform tasks that typically require human intelligence.

- *Machine Learning (ML):* A subset of AI where machines learn from data to make decisions.

- *Neural Networks (NN):* Digital brains made up of interconnected "neurons" that process data to learn tasks.

- *Deep Neural Networks (DNN):* More complex versions of neural networks with multiple layers for handling intricate tasks.

- *Convolutional Neural Networks (CNN):* Specialized neural networks for processing image data.

- *Generative Pre-trained Transformers (GPT):* AI models trained on vast amounts of text to generate humanlike text.

- *Large Language Models (LLM):* Advanced neural networks trained on extensive text data for understanding and generating language.

- *Retrieval Augmented Generation (RAG):* Combines retrieval of relevant information with AI's ability to generate answers.

Types of AI

- *Narrow AI:* Specialized for specific tasks, like setting alarms or identifying objects in photos.
- *Generative AI:* Creates new content based on existing data, such as generating text, images, or music.

How AI Works

1. *Data Collection (Ingredients):* AI needs high-quality data to function effectively.

2. *Algorithm (Recipe):* A set of instructions that guides AI on how to process data.

3. *Training (Taste Testing):* AI learns from data, adjusting its algorithms to improve accuracy.

4. *Prediction (Serving the Dish):* AI makes predictions based on new data.

5. *Testing and Validation (Feedback):* AI's predictions are tested to ensure accuracy, and feedback helps refine the algorithm.

6. *Optimization (Perfecting the Recipe):* Continuous learning and adjustments improve AI performance over time.

AI in Practice

AI is designed to handle tasks that are challenging or time-consuming for humans. It excels in areas where large amounts of data are involved, such as analyzing medical images or playing strategic games like Go and Chess. However, AI complements human abilities rather than replacing them, as it lacks human creativity, emotional intelligence, and contextual understanding.

Conclusion

AI is not magic but a powerful tool that, when properly understood and applied, can significantly enhance human capabilities. By embracing AI, individuals can focus on higher-value tasks that require a human touch, while AI handles more routine and data-intensive activities.

CHAPTER 4

Radiant Ascension: AI's Role in Personal Growth

It might seem strange to include this topic in a book that, to this point, has been all about digesting technical focal points of what AI is and how it is used in modern life, but I encourage you to stay focused on why you should care about AI's role in your life outside of work as much as its role in it.

To help keep this alignment, I want to open this discussion with the reason AI is a **very** important part of my own personal journey.

Throughout my teenage years, I struggled immensely with my own mind. I often had days where I'd lose control of my emotions or end up lost in my thoughts because I had no idea how to manage my consciousness.

In my early 20s, this only declined further as the world was smothered by COVID-19, and many other traumatic events in my life in sequence led me to feel like I was a victim of whatever my brain decided to put me through that day.

I know, little bit of a Debbie Downer, but trust me, this is all for a reason!

W. Hawkins, *AI Essentials Guide*, https://doi.org/10.1007/979-8-8688-0911-8_4

During this time, I was in my second year of a five-year bachelor's degree and took a course called Econometrics. In short, it's a class on how you can use statistical modelling to understand economic trends. For example, say you want to understand what causes people to get a divorce, you can model the likelihood of this event by mapping the relationships between the event and factors like income, occupation, number of children, etc.

This fundamentally changed the way I think. Learning that decisions like whether to separate from your partner or not could be modelled and understood through a variety of objective data points taught me that our minds are much less enigmatic than I wholeheartedly believed.

This was my introduction to AI, not ChatGPT, but the fundamentals of why the concept of AI is so valuable. Imagine you've built a model that uses this data to predict the likelihood of someone getting divorced and could provide explanations and recommendations to anyone you know as to why they are thinking about getting divorced. That is real, genuine, human impact technology. It may not save them from a nasty separation, and it may keep them stuck in a difficult marriage, but the potential of a machine, an AI model to supply that kind of guidance, changed my life.

This is why this matters, helping you understand why AI is so important to how you think and act may not provide you with a life-altering epiphany (hurt my ego a bit with that one), but it can help you see yourself a little bit differently.

Using AI to turn the daunting climb toward self-improvement into an inspiring journey of discovery, enhancement, and empowerment is no fairytale; it's a practical lifestyle choice.

I want to be honest; I had a difficult time figuring out how to approach writing this topic. There are so many ways to look at how AI factors into self-development especially as new tools powered by the latest advents make their way into the world.

I finally settled on the message of this chapter after a great conversation with my mom (a fellow techy). She shared what she was seeing in her world, particularly, how people later in their career were using the power of AI, and it was vastly different than the approach people in my circle and myself were taking to leveraging the technology.

Which is why we're having this conversation. As humans, we're all living and experiencing this explosion of innovation from our own unique perspective and will therefore react and interact with technological disruptions in completely idiosyncratic ways.

And that's exactly how it should be! However, I think some general guidance can transform this technological goldmine into a super charger that you can use to empower not only your productivity but your knowledge, your creativity, your critical thinking, and all the wonderful things that continue to separate us as an intelligent species growing and expanding with the world around us.

Ready to unlock your true potential?

Will: Alright, now that we have a pretty good understanding about AI, what it does, how it works, etc., how do you think it plays a role in how people become the best versions of themselves? What can it do for people right now to make their life better overall? I want the reader to really feel what AI offers as a vehicle of empowerment. Can you help me describe to them, at a fundamental level, how AI can help drive meaningful change in their lives?

Mira: Of course, Will. Let's approach this in a visceral, human-centric manner.

Imagine, dear reader, standing at the foot of a vast mountain—the mountain of your potential. It looms high, the peak shrouded in mists, signifying the best version of yourself: sharper mind, optimal health, and days bursting with productivity. The climb might seem daunting. But what if you had a guide, one that knows every nook and cranny, every cliff and passage of this mountain? This is what AI promises to be—your personal guide in this ascent.

- *A Beacon in the Fog of Learning: Remember those days when learning seemed a chore, where books were vast oceans that you were afraid to dive into? AI acts as the lighthouse, breaking down complex subjects into manageable bits, adapting to how YOU learn. It doesn't just throw information at you; it understands your rhythm, highlighting areas you excel at and patiently working with you on areas you struggle with.*

- *A Compass for Wellness: We've all been lost in the dense forest of health advice. "Eat this, not that." "Work out like this." But your body and mind are uniquely yours. AI understands that. It becomes a compass, pointing you to what truly works for you, whether it's a dietary change or a new exercise regime. It's like having a personal doctor and fitness coach in your pocket.*

- *The Time-Tamer: In the modern rush, hours slip like sand through fingers. With AI by your side, you're not just counting hours but making every hour count. It's the gentle whisper reminding you of appointments, the strategist that knows when you're most productive, the muse that suggests breaks when you're running on empty.*

AI doesn't just offer tools; it offers transformation. It's the alchemy that takes raw data—about how you learn, eat, work, and play—and turns it into gold: actionable insights tailored just for you. So, when we talk about AI driving meaningful change, it's about turning the impossible climb into an exhilarating journey, where every step, guided by intelligence, brings you closer to your peak.

In this era, AI is not just another tech buzzword. It's empowerment. It's a guide. And for those who embrace it, it's the wind beneath their wings in the flight to a better self.

Mira is definitely onto something here; in a very well-written article I stumbled across recently, David Johnston, a data scientist at Thoughtworks, puts it best:

> *AI is the field of study concerned with showing that things for which we thought required intelligence actually do not.*
>
> —David Johnston [1]

Meaning, they are things we do that can AND SHOULD be handled by a program. And, before you sharpen your pitchforks again, let me reiterate, I'm talking about the things you DON'T feel intelligent doing:

- Writing mundane emails
- Analyzing images
- Filling out forms or completing a checklist

Still want to lay on the sword of human superiority? What about all things we don't do intelligently when we SHOULD?

- Drive a car on less than six hours of sleep
- Inspect a very important piece of equipment we know nothing about
- Identify fire hazards

Alright, I'm not going to beat this drum any longer because those who don't get it probably weren't interested in hearing what I had to say anyways.

Now, let's talk about how to discern where AI fits into your world!

Will: Mira, if you were going to explain to the reader how they should approach using AI in their personal and professional life, what would you want them to know?

Mira: That's a thoughtful question, Will. If I were to advise readers on approaching AI in their lives, it would revolve around a few key principles:

- *Mindset of Curiosity: Embrace AI with an open mind and the curiosity of a child. This isn't just about adopting new tools; it's about embarking on a journey of exploration. As with any journey, there will be moments of wonder, moments of challenge, and countless opportunities to learn.*

Let's ground what Mira's suggesting. At a base level, you need to approach whatever aspect of AI you're tackling through the lens of an open mind.

If you've made it this far in the book, I doubt this will be a challenge for you to embrace, but it still cannot be stressed enough. It's easy to say you're open to the possibilities of AI, especially when it's all anyone's talking about but consistently exploring, learning, and forming opinions and knowledge on what AI stuff is valuable to your world and what's not is not so easy to discern.

Like any major tech advent before it, AI carries its own burden of risk. There will be people, companies, and organizations that bet on AI hard and lose, and there will be others that do the same and catapult their success to new stratospheres.

At the end of the day, if you accept the uncertainty of this new paradigm, you can never lose.

Better to do something imperfectly than to do nothing flaw- lessly—Robert Schuller.

- *AI As a Tool, Not a Crutch: Remember that AI is here to augment your abilities, not replace them. Use it as a powerful tool to enhance decision-making, productivity, and creativity. But also trust your intuition and human judgment. Machines provide data-driven insights; humans bring context, emotion, experience, and ethics into the equation.*

While percolating over what I wanted to write here, I spent a fair amount of time trying capture the message of this idea. How can I say, "Embrace AI and everything it brings!" without forewarning appropriate vs. inappropriate usage?

The best way to illustrate what is meant by "Use AI as a tool, not a crutch" is my own failures.

While working on one of my first major AI application projects, I quickly realized some of the parts of the app I understood clearly in concept were much more difficult to implement in reality (shocker, I know!).

I, of course, leveraged ChatGPT to fill in the knowledge gaps I needed to complete the project, but I noticed something very profound after a while of developing and troubleshooting.

There were times when the answer was RIGHT in front of me, but I would defer to my coding assistant to try and solve the problem.

This burned hours, days, even weeks of the project on things that were relatively simple to fix when I took a step back. And, moreover, I inevitably realized my reliance on the coding assistance was actually making the tool more of a hindrance than a value-add. As my mother beautifully pointed out when I talked about this experience:

There is nothing that replaces experience.

—Nancie Calder

You can have the most advanced, fancy, expensive AI tools at your disposal, but they still require human oversight. You can't use ChatGPT without writing a good prompt, you can't use GitHub Copilot without opening a code editor and knowing where to go from there, and you cannot accomplish your mission without bringing your own value to the table.

Yes, these tools can greatly increase your ability to create value, solve problems, and generate powerful solutions, but:

Without YOUR intelligence, there is NO intelligence.

- *Prioritize Privacy and Ethics: As AI becomes more integrated into daily tasks, be conscious of privacy concerns. Understand the data you're sharing and with whom. Choose platforms and tools that prioritize user data protection. Moreover, when using AI in decision-making, especially in professional settings, always consider the ethical implications of your actions.*

I don't think I'll ever be able to put it better than Stan Lee:

With great power comes great responsibility.

—Stan Lee

Sure, this probably seems like a cheesy nerd moment, but seriously, let's stop and think for a sec.

Most of us are no strangers to our species' history of taking advantage of so many things. People, equipment, resources; as great as we can be, we've undoubtedly brought a lot of harm and done some dark stuff while existing.

I'm not going to read you the riot act here, but it can't be stressed enough how important being cognizant, diligent, and responsible is when working, playing, experimenting, or doing anything that involves AI.

Thankfully, most of the big box solutions like ChatGPT, Microsoft Copilot, and Einstein have very sophisticated content moderation mechanisms, but we both know that's not going to stop everyone from misusing these newly democratized tools and the space they come from.

What I urge you and others entering this space to be aware of is exactly what's at stake: data and decisions.

In all cases, AI tools rely on data and large volumes of it. Make sure you are constantly questioning where the AI you're using is getting its data from; tools like M365 Copilot do an excellent job of helping users trust the information they receive by using data-grounding. This is a fancy term for providing sources you can click on to find where the chatbot got the information from.

If the AI tool you are using does not have a data-grounding mechanism you can use to validate the information it provides you, don't panic! That doesn't mean the AI you're using is untrustworthy, but you should definitely cross-reference Google or another information source you trust to validate you've got the facts.

That's the approach I've taken so far with Mira, and it's actually helped me find new, quality websites, authors, and other content hubs that have information that compliments what I'm looking for.

Of course, validating the model's output is only one-half of the puzzle. The choices and decisions you make with the results of this data and these models greatly determine the impact they have on the world around you.

Using AI to get and act on information is not a prescriptive service; you can't put the complete burden of an important personal or professional decision on a piece of software, no matter how convincing it may be. The AI software you're using doesn't have to deal with the moral, financial, social, emotional, and all other human implications of whether you choose A or B.

Your life, your responsibility.

All that being said, make sure you take the time to verify the value you're getting from these tools. It's not only important for your credibility but your safety and the safety of others whose information can be used by an AI. Take some of the time you're saving by using the tool to assess the impact of the activities you're conducting.

- *Continuous Learning and Adaptation: The world of AI is evolving rapidly. To harness its full potential, commit to continuous learning. Whether it's keeping up with the latest AI advancements or learning how to use a new AI-powered tool effectively, investing time in education will always yield returns.*

This is the fun part! The world of AI changes and expands so fast it's hard to keep track of. Yes, that may seem scary or difficult because you can't keep up with its pace, but there's no need to. As we've already explored, AI starts with data, and if you can master the fundamentals of data, AI, and their dynamic relationship with the world you operate in, you can't fall behind.

I know I've been good in this section at not being cliché, so apologies in advance for this next bit.

Working with new technologies is much like the tortoise and the hare, slow and steady wins the race! You can grab a hold of the latest and greatest and slingshot yourself into new futurist paradigms, but without the foundations of capturing, processing, and surfacing quality data and hooking that data up to a properly configured model, all which require time to be built, you're playing with volatile, expensive software that can create as many problems as solutions.

- *Harness AI's Power for Genuine Problems: It's easy to get caught up in the allure of AI and want to implement it everywhere. However, focus on areas where AI can*

*genuinely make a difference. Whether it's automating
mundane tasks, offering predictive insights, or
enhancing creativity, use AI where it truly adds value.*

One of the hardest things for most to decipher right now is not whether AI works for this or that but whether it should be used for this or that.

According to Forbes columnist, Barry Collins, people have asked tools like ChatGPT to do things ranging from building a magic potato to bringing down totalitarian regimes [2].

This goes back to an earlier point. AI is here to augment your abilities, not replace them. It is best suited for delegating mundane, routine tasks that take away from your ability to conduct high-value activities. That doesn't mean dump your baggage on the nearest chatbot in your proximity.

If you're looking for some kind of way to tell whether you should or shouldn't use AI in a situation, ask yourself these two questions:

1. Is what I'm asking this AI to do something I need done but can't afford to spend the time and/or energy on?

2. Can I easily determine whether the AI's output is accurate and valuable?

Deciding whether AI fits the task should be like handing your daily agenda to a personal assistant or intern, providing them the means to complete the tasks you don't have the capacity for but know exactly what the outcome should be.

- *Collaboration over Isolation: Remember, AI shines brightest when combined with human collaboration. In professional settings, encourage a culture where teams work alongside AI, understanding its strengths and weaknesses and leveraging its capabilities to drive collective success.*

Now that we're experiencing machines that can talk and act like humans, we need to be aware of how this affects our communication with friends, loved ones, colleagues, and everyone in between.

With more and more of our information-based interactions being with different Internet chat models, it's important to remember and value why humans are and have been the best source for help for other humans.

Yes, you can get a lot of very rich information from the Internet and/or chatbots, but they still don't and will probably never have the personalized experience and knowledge your friends, loved ones, and colleagues have that is most relevant to your journey.

I still remember trying to use ChatGPT for a WHOLE DAY to solve a problem with one of my work projects only to call my manager and have him show me what to do in 5 mins.

Thankfully, it wasn't a video call so he couldn't see the shades of embarrassment across every square inch of my face!

The people in your life are where the best information about your journey should lie. If that's not true, all I ask is you continue to search for those that value and support you as you are because there is no AI that can do that.

- *Embrace the Journey, Not Just the Destination: The real magic of AI is in the transformative journey it offers. It's not just about achieving a particular goal but about the myriad of ways it can reshape how you think, work, and grow. So, savor the process, learn from the missteps, and celebrate the milestones.*

With any new technology, it's important to recognize there can be a steep learning curve. Don't get discouraged if a tool you try doesn't work the way you expect it to or can't accomplish what you need it to.

A large part of using AI to elevate your personal growth journey is understanding and embracing that you are learning and changing just as the tools are and there will inevitably be bumps in the road of leveraging

AI to accomplish your self-development aspirations. If you're using a regression model to predict your split pace while training for a marathon, the quality of the prediction will only be as good as the number of timed runs you do. If you're using a writing assistant to pump out a new blog series, your ability to understand your audiences' changing appetites will dictate the quality of the content generated by the assistant.

Bottom line, if you take anything away from this chapter, it's this:

Using AI to grow requires you to grow too.

As you become stronger at providing the AI data, context, feedback, or other inputs and structuring your requests to fit your continuously refined objective, you will see a growing collaboration capability between you and the tool.

Microsoft minted the term Copilot for a reason; this journey you are on is about you, and as you change and evolve as a person, so will the AI tools' ability to elevate your value further and farther. You and AI are part of one feedback loop.

> *Will: Thank you, Mira. I'd like to close out this chapter with a list of questions the readers should be ready to ask themselves and others when deciding if, when, and how AI fits into the personal objective they are trying to accomplish. Can you help me craft those?*
>
> *Mira: Absolutely, Will. When contemplating the inclusion of AI into any personal or professional endeavor, asking the right questions is crucial. Here's a comprehensive list to guide readers in making informed decisions:*
>
> - *Purpose and Alignment*
>   - *What specific problem or challenge am I hoping AI will address?*
>   - *How does incorporating AI align with my larger goals or objectives?*

- *Value Addition*

  - *In what tangible ways can I see AI enhancing or improving the task at hand?*

  - *Are there areas where AI might overcomplicate the process or add unnecessary layers?*

- *Data and Privacy*

  - *What kind of data will the AI need to function effectively? How will my data be stored, processed, and protected?*

  - *Are there any potential ethical or privacy concerns associated with using this data?*

- *Accessibility and Usability*

  - *How user-friendly is the AI solution? Will there be a steep learning curve?*

  - *Are there resources or training available to help me better understand and utilize the AI system?*

- *Integration*

  - *How seamlessly can this AI solution integrate into my current workflow or lifestyle?*

  - *Will I need additional tools or platforms to make it work effectively?*

- *Feedback and Adaptability*

  - *How does the AI solution handle feedback? Can it learn and adapt over time based on my needs?*

  - *Is there an option to recalibrate or fine-tune its responses or recommendations?*

- *Ethical and Social Implications*
  - *Are there potential unintended consequences of using this AI in my context?*
  - *How might the adoption of this AI impact those around me, both positively and negatively?*

I hope this chapter has illuminated, in some regard, how AI can play a part in your everyday activities and that, with the right principles, mindset, and action, it can act as a catapult that launches your ability to be the best version of you to the next level.

Of course, the realization of that value all comes down to who you are. Let's end things off with a quote that really captures the essence of the relationship of AI and personal growth:

AI is a tool. The choice how it gets deployed is ours.

—Oren Etzioni

Summary: Radiant Ascension
AI As a Tool for Self-improvement

AI can transform the journey of self-improvement into an inspiring adventure by providing personalized support in various aspects:

- *Learning:* AI breaks down complex subjects into manageable bits, adapting to individual learning styles and highlighting areas for improvement.
- *Wellness:* AI offers personalized health advice, acting as a personal doctor and fitness coach tailored to individual needs.

- *Productivity:* AI helps manage time effectively, reminding of appointments, suggesting breaks, and identifying peak productivity times.

Guidance on Embracing AI

To harness AI's potential for personal growth, the author provides several key principles:

1. *Mindset of Curiosity:* Embrace AI with an open mind and a willingness to explore and learn continuously.

2. *AI As a Tool, Not a Crutch:* Use AI to augment abilities, not replace them. Trust human intuition and judgment alongside AI's data-driven insights.

3. *Prioritize Privacy and Ethics:* Be conscious of privacy concerns, understand the data being shared, and consider the ethical implications of AI use.

4. *Continuous Learning and Adaptation:* Commit to ongoing education about AI advancements to stay updated and make informed decisions.

5. *Genuine Problem-Solving:* Focus on areas where AI can genuinely add value and enhance productivity, creativity, and decision-making.

6. *Collaboration over Isolation:* Combine human collaboration with AI's strengths for collective success in professional settings.

7. *Embrace the Journey:* Recognize the transformative journey AI offers and enjoy the process of learning and growing with AI.

Key Questions to Consider

When deciding if, when, and how to incorporate AI into personal or professional life, consider the following questions:

- *Purpose and Alignment:* What specific problem is AI addressing? How does it align with larger goals?

- *Value Addition:* How will AI enhance the task? Will it overcomplicate processes?

- *Data and Privacy:* What data is required? How is it stored and protected? Are there ethical concerns?

- *Accessibility and Usability:* Is the AI user-friendly? Are resources available for learning?

- *Integration:* How seamlessly can AI integrate into current workflows? Are additional tools needed?

- *Feedback and Adaptability:* How does AI handle feedback and adapt over time? Can it be recalibrated?

- *Ethical and Social Implications:* What are the unintended consequences? How does AI adoption impact others?

Conclusion

AI can play a significant role in personal growth by providing tools for learning, wellness, and productivity. By embracing AI with the right mindset and principles, individuals can use it to enhance their abilities and achieve personal goals. The journey of integrating AI into personal development is ongoing, requiring continuous learning, ethical considerations, and a focus on genuine problem-solving.

CHAPTER 5

Guided by the Constellation: Navigating the Business Galaxy of AI

Imagine having a north star to follow when planning the future success of your business. This chapter will show you how AI can be used as a navigator to steer toward unexplored horizons of opportunity and success.

As an entrepreneur and innovation consultant, I've grown up thinking and creating things I thought other people would love because I loved them.

When I was seven or eight, while having a family dinner at a restaurant, I came up with the brilliant idea of breadtons. If the term doesn't mean anything to you, I think it will make complete sense with this imagery.

Imagine you are the parent of a seven-year-old and in the middle of having dinner, you glance over to see your seven-year-old shoving croutons into a piece of garlic toast. You ask, "Hey, what are you doing?" and, with a patronizing tone, they respond, "I'm making breadtons." You stare for a moment, pondering how does anyone respond to this kind of statement. Eventually, you come to realize that breadtons is a very fitting description for croutons smushed into garlic bread. You admit to yourself those would be **absolutely** delicious and move to the more pressing matter. Is this kid a genius or a sociopath?

I am certain this is the exact reaction my mother, father, and grandfather had as they actively watched me devour this tasty treat (and none of my veggies, big surprise!) because what garlic bread and crouton connoisseur wouldn't enjoy the two powerhouses together.

Sadly, the success of my breadton invention was short-lived as a similar snack, Grissol's baguettes snack, hit our family grocery cart shortly after. I, of course, did not and still don't have the resources to fight a patent battle on this front. Begrudgingly, I admit I have eaten these copycats quite a few times and loved every nibble so the patent war wouldn't have much bite to it anyways, pun intended.

I did, however, learn something very valuable from that experiment and many others over the years:

You have to create something that makes a difference to make a difference.

This is the premise for my business philosophy and what I will rely on to get my message across in this chapter. This is the what; let's breakdown the why and the how.

> *Will: Mira, the "creator economy" was estimated to be worth 104.2 billion in mid-2022 [1]. It's clear to see that the world's markets are converging towards a reality where organic, valuable, and ever-expanding solutions are the competitive advantage in any industry. What do you think is the role of AI in this transformation? Fundamentally, what do you think AI offers businesses in relation to their future?*

> *Mira: That's an insightful observation, Will. The creator economy's growth signals a broader trend: the shift from traditional, top-down production models to decentralized, community-driven ones. In this new paradigm, individual creativity and niche expertise are celebrated, leading to more personalized and contextually relevant solutions.*

AI plays a multifaceted role in this transformation:

- *Scalability: While individual creators bring unique value, they often lack the scale of traditional corporations. AI can bridge this gap. For instance, personalized content recommendations, AI-generated designs, or even AI-composed music can allow individual creators to cater to a larger, diverse audience without diluting their core message or aesthetic.*

- *Personalization: AI excels at processing large datasets and identifying patterns. This means it can offer hyper-personalized experiences, ensuring consumers get content, products, or services tailored specifically to their preferences, improving engagement and loyalty.*

- *Efficiency: Many creators wear multiple hats— from content creation to marketing to business administration. AI tools can automate repetitive tasks, streamline workflows, and provide actionable insights, allowing creators to focus on what they do best: creating.*

- *Informed Decision-Making: Data-driven insights powered by AI can help businesses spot trends, understand audience preferences, and adapt in real time. This ensures businesses stay relevant and agile in the ever-evolving landscape.*

- *Democratization of Tools: AI-powered platforms have reduced the entry barrier for many sectors. From AI-assisted video editing to AI-driven market research, tools that were once exclusive to big corporations are now accessible to individual creators.*

Fundamentally, AI offers businesses a chance to be both vast and intimate—vast in scale and reach, yet intimate in understanding and serving each customer's unique needs. It merges the efficiency and power of technology with the nuance and authenticity of human creativity. In the context of the future, AI positions businesses to be adaptable, informed, and exceptionally attuned to the evolving desires of their audience. It's not just about being technologically advanced; it's about being profoundly human-centric in an increasingly digital age.

Entrepreneurial futurist, Andrew Griffiths, famously said in one of his books that

The business landscape has evolved. Being around for a while no longer cuts it. If anything, people see companies that have been around for a while as old and stuffy.

I think most business leaders or owners have grown to understand this paradigm shift in the last four years with the fallout of the COVID-19 pandemic.

The pandemic brought with it many things but nothing more profound than its effect on the pace of change we all experience as humans.

For businesses, if you did not have an online presence or digital payment solutions, there's a good chance you went under and went under fast. Larger corporations had to pivot resources from office furniture to Zoom or Teams licenses, and what used to be a simple, straightforward landscape of commerce activity did seven backflips all at once and became the digital economy we all participate in today.

A 2020 McKinsey survey of executives found that the majority of leaders have seen an accelerated digitization of their customer and supply chain interactions and of their internal operations by three to four years [2].

Additionally, the share of digital or digitally enabled products in their portfolios has accelerated by a shocking seven years [3], and another survey they conducted of consumers showed that respondents are three times likelier now than before the crisis to say that at least 80% of their customer interactions are digital in nature [4].

Meaning, whether you like it or not, digital transformation is here to stay and accelerating at a rapid pace. More importantly, your company's digital footprint carries much more weight than you may realize.

To me, this is where the AI-in-business conversation really begins. Not with chatbots or digital art or prompting but with the fundamentals: data.

Through all the wildly fascinating movements of the digital economy and AI in the last four years, there has been one constant.

Data is the beating heart of all of it.

You're more likely to order something on Uber Eats you've ordered before because of data. Your daily news is crawling with studies, percentages, counts, and tables. When most of us hear "data," I don't think we really grasp the brevity of what that term entails.

Data is all information collected and acted on in our daily lives.

We're using data to make decisions on our diet, our children's laundry, and even when we go to the bathroom. These may seem like obscure examples, but they are reality.

We're in an age where any information you could possibly want is at your fingertips. You can find new, fun, healthy recipes on Pinterest in a three-second scroll. You can learn about the pros and cons of 19 different detergent brands with a few Google searches, and you can read a study per hour on whether coffee does or does not cause cancer, depending on how much caffeine you're running on.

The point is, we're living, breathing, and absorbing data in so many forms all the time that it makes perfect sense that it is at the heart of the way we invest our time, energy, and money in different products and services.

Another McKinsey study (they are having a day today!) found that data-driven organizations are...ready?...

23 TIMES MORE LIKELY TO ACQUIRE CUSTOMERS

Twenty...Three!

And it doesn't stop there; those same organizations are six times more likely to retain customers and 19 TIMES more likely to be more profitable [5].

To be honest, I could end this chapter here, and I think all would need to be said as to why AI is relevant in your business, but let's look at what this looks like in practice.

Data drives understanding. Understanding turns into knowledge. Knowledge guides decisions. Decisions dictate actions, and meaningful, insightful action creates a stronger bond with your customers and/or clients which results in better business outcomes.

To me, this is the biggest differentiator between a business and a great business. Leveraging data shows you are resourceful, considerate, and actually give care about how your customers experience your products, services, and organization. It's really that simple.

But that doesn't make it easy, and that is largely why I stress the importance of getting on the data-driven bandwagon as soon as you finish reading this section.

There are too many organizations that haphazardly collect and store different kinds of poorly kept data then try to layer AI on top of it and expect it to magically do everything you expect it to and more.

This will fail, royally, every...time

Why? I am so glad you asked. Why is building quality datasets to enact smarter business decisions so important?

Outside of this being a rhetorical question, let's see exactly why data-driven business isn't just the future but the present and the actual foundation for making progress with AI in your business.

In 2012 [6], before Netflix was Netflix, they purchased two full seasons of *House of Cards* for $100M—without seeing a single episode. Why?

The company saw that fans of the original UK *House of Cards* also watched movies that starred Kevin Spacey and were directed by David Fincher, one of the show's executive producers.

Combining these elements with a stellar writing and production team created a recipe for success. The show immediately took off, with some indicating they would maintain their Netflix subscription for the sole purpose of watching *House of Cards*.

Now a major arm of its business, Netflix original content is heavily informed not just by its own user data, but by trends the team sees on social media, viewership in competing markets, and running predictive algorithms that draw correlations between elements of high-performing content—looking at combinations of talent, storylines, themes, and directors.

Every decision made at Netflix is deeply driven by data. According to a presentation by Jeff Magnusson, manager of data platform architecture at Netflix, and engineer Charles Smith, the brand's data philosophy encompasses three key tenets:

1. Data should be accessible, easy to discover, and easy to process for everyone.

2. Whether your dataset is large or small, being able to visualize it makes it easier to explain.

3. The longer you take to find the data, the less valuable it becomes.

The third principle specifically sticks out in our discussion; the longer you take to create efficient and effective data collection systems, management processes, and systems for presenting the information clearly, the less valuable it is.

This is because of many things but mainly because of data drift which is the phenomenon of data becoming less relevant and accurate as time goes on because of the constantly evolving landscape our business operates in.

Which brings me to the absolute crux of this conversation:

Using data (and by proxy, AI) in your business is an ITERATIVE process.

You have to create a feedback loop of collecting, organizing, analyzing, and acting on the data available to you if you stand a chance of ever leveraging data and AI to grow your business and make better decisions.

To be totally cliché, it's kind of like growing a prize-winning garden. You can't just snap your fingers and be flush with shrubbery. You plant the seeds, you check the seeds, you water the seeds, you trim the plants as they grow, and repeat.

This is because data and AI are all pattern driven, meaning you need enough time and repetition to have the pattern materialize.

And the feedback loop is what creates the lessons and momentum you need to transform your business into a place where you can capitalize on these tools.

Like any road to a goal, the path is a system of small, consistent steps that provide you with the intel and experience to align your trajectory and clear your direction to the completion of the goal. And the more consistent and intentional you get, the shorter your trajectory to the target becomes.

Let me be clear; I'm not saying to go scrape, crawl, and download every piece of business data at your disposal. What I want you to do today is this:

Identify a problem in your organization you wish you had more information on. Can be as big as your customer churn rate or as small as optimizing the office snack stock.

Now that you've identified what data you want, you need to identify what data you have access to. In the case of the office snack stock, can you get access to POs and internal surveys on employee preferences or maybe you simply start by having people jot down what they eat and what they don't (for observation, not judgement of course).

Once you've collected some data, how do you want to organize it? Is it easier for you to read a table, a chart, or some fancy infographic? The medium doesn't matter as long as you can interpret what you create.

Now for the fun part! What patterns can you find? Maybe you find people are eating more of the complimentary licorice in October, or the breakfast bar supply depletes faster during the end of your company's fiscal year. Bottom line, what does the data tell you and how can you use that information to influence the outcome of the problem? Maybe it's ordering double the amount of breakfast bars a week before the year-end deadline or ordering more fruits and veggies after Christmas holidays.

Once you've implemented your changes, repeat the process. Collect, assess, and try something different.

Voila! You are now a data-driven decision-maker; congratulations!

I can understand if I'm coming across facetious or patronizing, but I really want to illuminate how simple, but important, this habit can be.

As we've discussed earlier on, there is no AI model without the data properly modelled, managed, and organized so you have to start with building good data decision-making habits. It is these abilities combined with you or your company's deep understanding of the subject matter of the data (e.g., supply chain, finance, patient records) that produces the opportunity to build AI that are impactful, thoughtful, useful, and uniquely valuable.

Of course, this applies for the AI models you stack on top of your data model as well. Machine learning, using LLMs and any other AI use case, is just as iterative as the data-driven feedback loop. You identify a problem that could possibly benefit from AI, select and try a model, examine the results, and then decide on the next step from there.

If this process seems difficult, I promise it only gets easier. Using these tools is a muscle, and you will be surprised by not only the impact working them has on you and your business but also by how fast it takes to see a prominent impact.

Because, at the end of the day,

Using data and AI in business successfully is about two things: lessons and momentum.

You need a clear system for creating meaningful lessons in understanding your organization (i.e., data collection, interpretation, and analysis), and you need to act on this understanding consistently to produce momentum that carry you to the results you seek.

Nevertheless, we are discussing using AI in business so I would be remise if I did not provide an action plan for how you can get started with taking this knowledge to the challenges your organization is facing today.

The Framework

Throughout my conversations with clients and actually implementing AI in practice, there are three key tenets that I pay attention to when assessing whether AI is a good fit for a particular challenge an organization is looking to solve.

Finding the Pain Points

I'm sure you've come across some of the stock examples like an email writer or a bot that schedules things for you or sends reminders to teammates, but at the core of all of these scenarios is the same principle:

In knowledge work, when you agree to a new commitment, whether it's a small task or a big project, it brings with it a certain amount of ongoing administrative overhead. This overhead produces a compounding tax that chews at more and more of an individual's mental bandwidth as their responsibilities grow [7].

This can look like being stuck in meetings explaining procedures and policies to new hires or gathering disparate data from departmental silos to create executive reports. It can even just be facilitating an effective strategy meeting focused on creating new lines of business to pursue in the next fiscal year.

In all of these cases and many others similar, it is the drain of your mental bandwidth from cognitively intensive tasks that are rote, mindless, and absorbing but absolutely need to get done.

These are the areas to find within your or your customer's organization because they provide the greatest chance to drive a real, tangible impact in using AI to change the way your workforce or customers operate.

Assessing these pain points not only provides a chance to increase the efficiency and efficacy of your employees or customers but also creates an opportunity to improve the work they do.

When you've identified the leeches on their bandwidth and what eats at their day, you're freeing them up to do the actual deep, important work they do with greater focus, intention, and quality which has been proven to provide numerous individual, departmental, and organizational benefits.

For example, when Lotta Laitinen, a manager at If, a Scandinavian insurance company (`https://www.if-insurance.com/about-if/about-us.`), jettisoned meetings and administrative tasks in order to spend more time supporting her team, it led to a 5% increase in sales by her unit over a three-week period [8].

Reinventing the Process

It's not just about identifying the pain points but correcting them too. When implementing AI systems, you cannot just overlay a model on top of a process that wasn't working in the first place.

Identifying, ideating, and thinking critically on what needs to be changed within the process is largely where the distinction of using AI comes from. When you are able to identify exactly where the bottlenecks are in your process, you can effectively explore how AI can relieve those points of contention.

For example, say you are the manager of a small enterprise resource planning (ERP) consulting company; your consultants require your approval of all expenses they submit on their timesheet. Of course, you're very busy with important things like creating request for proposal (RFP) responses, putting together reports for leadership, and planning customer events for the next quarter so the time you can put toward reviewing the consultants' expenditures is limited.

The bottleneck, in this case, would be the need to review all line items of the expenses spreadsheet when you're really just looking for any that require clarification with the submitter.

So, rather than having an AI model that is instructed to examine each line item of the spreadsheet, the AI should be instructed to simply identify any items that do not clearly align with the organization's policies and procedures. This way, anything important that requires your review is flagged, and rather than chewing up bandwidth looking at everything, you only have to examine a few key items and make sure they can be approved.

The main idea is you have to identify how the process can be improved before considering what role the AI model will play. Often, the challenge with implementing AI effectively is not necessarily an issue with the model but the situation it is being asked to assist with.

This also provides the chance to understand the cause of the inefficiency and how that can be addressed at a larger level within the organization. You may find that what seemed like a tiny inefficiency in how expense paperwork is handled may be part of some larger inconsistency with company policies and procedures.

Reinforcing the Human in the Loop

Central to this framework is the belief that AI should amplify, not replace, human intelligence. By taking over rote tasks, AI gives the human operator the space to excel in areas requiring critical thinking, discernment, and creative work.

Of course, this offers numerous benefits to individuals and their organizations, but this does not mean that individuals can be removed completely from the task. Not only for dependency, safety, and ethical reasons but for the sake of learning and development, both for the AI models deployed and the individuals they work with.

For example, radiologists leverage computer vision (a type of machine learning) to identify cancerous cells at a higher level of accuracy than humans, but they are still the decision-maker as to what operations, treatments, and medication to offer to patients for obvious ethical and legal reasons.

But this processor–decision-maker relationship has ancillary benefits. Radiologists can learn what AI models are able to see that makes them able to identify problems with higher precision, and the radiologists, of course, continue to provide feedback and evaluate AI inferences so that the AI model continues to improve its accuracy further and further as well.

What many struggle to realize with AI, and for that matter, any emerging technology, is that the journey of practically implementing the tool is an iterative process. The machine learns from human feedback, and humans learn how to use the machine by trying it out and using it in constructed situations.

This, of course, only occurs when the humans remain in the loop. When things are completely automated, there is no chance for continuous improvement. The model receives very little constructive feedback because the decision-makers are not engaged with its application, and this lack of engagement also keeps the decision-makers from improving their own understanding of the process outcomes which may be critical for other, higher-value work that an AI cannot do well.

When the focus of the AI implementation is maximizing the impact of the human in the loop rather than how to replace them, the organization, the individuals, and the machines that have begun to enter their ecosystem all benefit in an equitable and more prominent way. The sum of all parts is always greater than the value of any individual component.

The Framework in Action

Now that we've grasped what is important in creating a framework that maximizes the benefits AI brings to your organization, let's see what this looks like in action.

Here's a little story [9]:

A few years ago, an unnamed Fortune 500 company decided to adopt an earlier version of OpenAI's ChatGPT.

This company provides other companies with administrative software. Think like programs that help businesses do accounting and logistics. A big part of this company's job is helping its customers, mostly small businesses, with technical support.

The company's customer support agents are based primarily in the Philippines, but also in the United States and other countries. And they spend their days helping small businesses tackle various kinds of technical problems with their software. Think like, "Why am I getting this error message?" or "Help! I can't log in!"

Instead of talking to their customers on the phone, these customer service agents mostly communicate with them through online chat windows. These troubleshooting sessions can be quite long. The average conversation between the agents and customers lasts about 40 minutes. Agents need to know the ins and outs of their company's software, how to solve problems, and how to deal with sometimes irate customers. It's a stressful job, and there's high turnover. In the broader customer service industry, up to 60% [10] of reps quit each year.

Facing such high turnover rates, this software company was spending a lot of time and money training new staffers. And so, in late 2020, it decided to begin using an AI system to help its constantly churning customer support staff get better at their jobs faster. The company's goal was to improve the performance of their workers, not replace them.

Now, when the agents look at their computer screens, they don't only see a chat window with their customers. They also see another chat window with an AI chatbot, which is there to help them more effectively assist customers in real time. It advises them on what to potentially write to customers and also provides them with links to internal company information to help them more quickly find solutions to their customers' technical problems.

This interactive chatbot was trained by reading through a ton of previous conversations between reps and customers. It has recognized word patterns in these conversations, identifying key phrases and common problems facing customers and how to solve them. Because the company tracks which conversations leave its customers satisfied, the AI chatbot also knows formulas that often lead to success. Think, like, interactions that customers give a five-star rating. "I'm so sorry you're frustrated with error message 504. All you have to do is restart your computer and then press Ctrl-Alt-Shift. Have a blessed day!"

After the software company adopted AI, the average customer support representative became, on average, 14% more productive. They were able to resolve more customer issues per hour. That's huge. The company's workforce is now much faster and more effective. They're also, apparently, happier. Turnover has gone down, especially among new hires.

Not only that, but the company's customers also are more satisfied. They give higher ratings to support staff. They also generally seem to be nicer in their conversations and are less likely to ask to speak to an agent's supervisor.

Conclusion

This chapter may not have been what you were expecting to hear about using AI in business, but it is what I believe you need to hear. At the end of the day, you can try a million different out-of-the-box AI products or try building your own AI systems, but until you've created a system for managing, understanding, and utilizing your organizational data and how an AI model interacts with that data, there's really not much you can benefit from.

Moreover, your system for assessing, evaluating, critically thinking, and implementing an AI solution into an existing workflow needs to be more than "let's throw AI at it." Not only for return on investment (ROI) reasons but for the change management, sustainability, infrastructure, development, training, education, and many other aspects of bringing any solution to life. You need to be intentional, thoughtful, and bold with how you craft your AI framework. We'll discuss this more when we get to AI governance methods.

That being said, once you've put in the work to acquire and use the right data with the right AI models in the right scenarios with the right methodologies, your or your customer's organization will literally, and I really mean this, transform.

Summary: Guided by the Constellation

Introduction

This chapter explores how AI can serve as a guiding star for businesses, steering them toward new opportunities and success. It emphasizes the importance of creating impactful innovations and leveraging AI to enhance business operations.

The Creator Economy and AI

The creator economy, valued at over $100 billion in 2022, represents a shift toward decentralized, community-driven production models. AI plays a crucial role in this transformation by offering:

- *Scalability:* AI enables creators to reach larger audiences without compromising their core values.

- *Personalization:* AI processes large datasets to provide hyper-personalized experiences.

- *Efficiency:* AI automates repetitive tasks, allowing creators to focus on their strengths.

- *Informed Decision-Making:* AI offers data-driven insights to help businesses stay relevant and agile.

- *Democratization of Tools:* AI-powered platforms make advanced tools accessible to individual creators.

The Importance of Data Quality

Data is the foundation of the digital economy and AI applications. It drives understanding, which translates into knowledge, guiding decisions, and actions that strengthen customer relationships and business outcomes. Data-driven organizations are significantly more likely to acquire and retain customers and be profitable.

Implementing AI in Business

Effective AI implementation requires a systematic approach, focusing on:

- *Finding Pain Points:* Identify areas where mental bandwidth is drained by routine tasks. Addressing these areas can improve efficiency and quality of work.

- *Reinventing Processes:* Before deploying AI, reassess and improve existing processes. AI should enhance, not simply overlay, existing workflows.

- *Reinforcing Human Involvement:* AI should amplify human intelligence, not replace it. Maintaining human oversight ensures continuous improvement and ethical considerations.

Case Study: AI in Customer Support

A Fortune 500 company implemented AI to assist customer support agents, resulting in a 14% increase in productivity and improved customer satisfaction. The AI chatbot provided real-time assistance and access to internal information, helping agents resolve issues more efficiently.

Conclusion

Using AI in business is an iterative process that requires a clear system for managing data and integrating AI solutions effectively. A thoughtful, intentional approach to AI can transform organizations by enhancing decision-making, improving efficiency, and fostering innovation. The chapter underscores the need for businesses to adopt data-driven practices and continuously refine their AI strategies to achieve lasting success.

CHAPTER 6

Navigating the Shadows: The Ethical Maze of AI

It's time to identify where the bright promise of this technology meets the intricate challenges of moral choices. This chapter reveals the delicate balance between innovation and responsibility, guiding you through the nuanced paths where AI's potential is weighed against its pitfalls.

When I was in my late teenage years, I went through a very profound and difficult period of time I would still consider to be the "rock bottom" of my life. I was close to failing my second year of a five-year applied math degree, I had negative 2 dollars to my name (literally), I was working two crummy jobs to cover my expenses, I was going through a messy split from my longest-ever relationship at the time, and I had also recently received a troubling health diagnosis that shook much of the foundation of my self-perception.

The reason I mention this is because it was the first time I diligently had to find the positives in an otherwise negative circumstance, and it taught me a lot about perceptions and that there is always a dichotomy in how we as humans see situations in our world.

W. Hawkins, *AI Essentials Guide*, https://doi.org/10.1007/979-8-8688-0911-8_6

It is that fundamental truth that guided me through the world's first modern pandemic, the rest of my degree, and countless other life obstacles I've faced along the way.

The reason this fundamental truth is so important and relevant in our conversation is because it is the most prominent way, I've found, to remain holistically aware of the intricacies of any event, idea, or piece of reality that plays a part in our overall life satisfaction.

Understanding that the nature of everything is to contain a balance of positive and negative energy is the premise for any conversation about the challenges and ethical considerations of AI and using it in life and business.

As amazing and impactful as the technology is, there is no doubt it can and has been misused in many cases, and there are consequences associated with that.

Here's a shortlist, compiled by Thor Olavsrud at CIO [1] of notable AI disasters in recent years. I'm including this information not to fearmonger or advocate against the use of the technology but to bring awareness to the implications of its misuse and, moreover, to bring a holistic understanding of exactly what's at stake when using this technology.

1. *ChatGPT Hallucinates Court Cases*

    Steven A. Schwartz, an attorney with Levidow & Oberman, used the OpenAI generative AI chatbot to find prior cases to support a case filed by Colombian airline Avianca employee Roberto Mata for injuries he sustained in 2019. The only problem? At least six of the cases submitted in the brief did not exist.

    In a document filed in May 2023, Judge Castel noted the cases submitted by Schwartz included false names and docket numbers, along with bogus internal citations and quotes.

In an affidavit, Schwartz told the court that it was the first time he had used ChatGPT as a legal research source, and he was "unaware of the possibility that its content could be false." He admitted that he had not confirmed the sources provided by the AI chatbot. He also said that he "greatly regrets having utilized generative artificial intelligence to supplement the legal research performed herein and will never do so in the future without absolute verification of its authenticity."

In June 2023, Judge Castel imposed a $5,000 fine on Schwartz.

2. *Zillow Slashed Workforce Due to Failure of Home-Buying Algorithm*

In November 2021, online real estate marketplace Zillow told shareholders it would wind down its Zillow Offers operations and cut 25% of the company's workforce—about 2,000 employees—over the next several quarters.

The home-flipping unit's woes were the result of the error rate in the machine learning algorithm it used to predict home prices. Zillow Offers was a program through which the company made cash offers on properties based on a "Zestimate" of home values derived from a machine learning algorithm.

The idea was to renovate the properties and flip them quickly. But a Zillow spokesperson told CNN that the algorithm had a median error rate of 1.9%, and the error rate could be much higher, as much as 6.9%, for off-market homes.

CNN reported that Zillow bought 27,000 homes through Zillow Offers since its launch in April 2018 but sold only 17,000 through the end of September 2021. Black swan events like the COVID-19 pandemic and a home renovation labor shortage contributed to the algorithm's accuracy troubles. Zillow said the algorithm had led it to unintentionally purchase homes at higher prices than its current estimates of future selling prices, resulting in a $304 million inventory write-down in Q3 2021.

3. *Healthcare Algorithm Failed to Flag Black Patients*

In 2019, a study published in *Science* revealed that a healthcare prediction algorithm, used by hospitals and insurance companies throughout the United States to identify patients in need of "high-risk care management" programs, was far less likely to single out Black patients.

High-risk care management programs provide trained nursing staff and primary care monitoring to chronically ill patients in an effort to prevent serious complications. But the algorithm was much more likely to recommend White patients for these programs than Black patients.

The study found that the algorithm used healthcare spending data as a proxy for determining an individual's healthcare need. But according to *Scientific American*, the healthcare costs of sicker Black patients were on par with the costs of healthier White people, which meant they received lower risk scores even when their need was greater.

4. *Dataset Trained Microsoft Chatbot to Spew Racist Tweets*

In March 2016, Microsoft learned that using Twitter interactions as training data for machine learning algorithms can have dismaying results.

Microsoft released Tay, an AI chatbot, on the social media platform. The company described it as an experiment in "conversational understanding." The idea was that the chatbot would assume the persona of a teen girl and interact with individuals via Twitter using a combination of machine learning and natural language processing. Microsoft seeded it with anonymized public data and some material pre-written by comedians and then set it loose to learn and evolve from its interactions on the social network.

What Microsoft didn't take into account was that a group of Twitter users would immediately begin tweeting racist and misogynist comments to Tay. The bot quickly learned from that material and incorporated it into its own tweets.

Within 16 hours, the chatbot posted more than 95,000 tweets, and those tweets rapidly turned overtly racist, misogynist, and anti-Semitic. Microsoft quickly suspended the service for adjustments and ultimately pulled the plug.

"We are deeply sorry for the unintended offensive and hurtful tweets from Tay, which do not represent who we are or what we stand for, nor how we designed Tay," Peter Lee, corporate vice president,

Microsoft Research and Incubations (then corporate vice president of Microsoft Healthcare), wrote in a post on Microsoft's official blog following the incident.

5. *Amazon AI-Enabled Recruitment Tool Only Recommended Men*

In 2014, Amazon started working on AI-powered recruiting software to do just that. There was only one problem: The system vastly preferred male candidates.

In 2018, Reuters broke the news that Amazon had scrapped the project. Amazon's system gave candidates star ratings from one to five. But the machine learning models at the heart of the system were trained on 10 years' worth of resumes submitted to Amazon—most of them from men.

As a result of that training data, the system started penalizing phrases in the resume that included the word "women's" and even downgraded candidates from all-women colleges.

At the time, Amazon said the tool was never used by Amazon recruiters to evaluate candidates. The company tried to edit the tool to make it neutral but ultimately decided it could not guarantee it would not learn some other discriminatory way of sorting candidates and ended the project.

6. *Target Analytics Violated Privacy*

In 2012, an analytics project by retail titan Target showcased how much companies can learn about customers from their data. According to the *New York Times*, in 2002, Target's marketing department started wondering how it could determine whether customers are pregnant.

That line of inquiry led to a predictive analytics project that would famously lead the retailer to inadvertently reveal to a teenage girl's family that she was pregnant. That, in turn, would lead to all manner of articles and marketing blogs citing the incident as part of advice for avoiding the "creepy factor."

Target's marketing department wanted to identify pregnant individuals because there are certain periods in life—pregnancy foremost among them—when people are most likely to radically change their buying habits.

If Target could reach out to customers in that period, it could, for instance, cultivate new behaviors in those customers, getting them to turn to Target for groceries or clothing or other goods.

Like all other big retailers, Target had been collecting data on its customers via shopper codes, credit cards, surveys, and more. It mashed that data up with demographic data and third-party data it purchased. Crunching all that data enabled Target's analytics team to determine that there were about 25 products sold by Target that could be analyzed together to generate a "pregnancy prediction" score.

The marketing department could then target high-scoring customers with coupons and marketing messages.

Additional research would reveal that studying customers' reproductive status could feel creepy to some of those customers. According to the *Times*, the company didn't back away from its targeted marketing but did start mixing in ads for things they knew pregnant women wouldn't buy—including ads for lawn mowers next to ads for diapers—to make the ad mix feel random to the customer.

These six incidents should help relieve some paranoia about any kind of AI armageddon since the consequences of all the events did not result in any world-ending harm, but the consequences are, nonetheless, consequences and effect real people in real ways.

That being said, what do you notice these six stories have in common? In each case, the incident occurred because of two factors: issues with the data and human error.

AI algorithms that produce biased, unfair, unjust, discriminatory, disturbing, or inappropriate outputs are a result of a concept known as AI bias, a phenomenon that occurs when an algorithm produces results that are systemically prejudiced due to erroneous assumptions in the machine learning (ML) process [2].

In the legal research story, it was Schwartz's assumption that every response returned by the model was entirely and thoroughly accurate. In the Zillow story, it was the company's inability to accommodate for high variance in the model's training data. In the healthcare algorithm story, it was the developer's inability to identify the bias in the healthcare spending data. In the Microsoft chatbot story, it was the developer's failure to realize the sheer stupidity of Twitter trolls.

AI is a great tool that can do many great things when approached correctly and a lot of terrible things when misused. It's like a hammer; the ethical nature of it is sheerly determined by what it's swung at.

Except, AI (and it's bias) is much more complicated than a hammer.

Will: Mira, what would you say are the most prominent mistakes people make that result in AI bias?

Mira: Several factors, often rooted in human error or oversight, contribute to the emergence of bias in AI systems:

- *Biased Training Data: This is perhaps the most common source of AI bias. If the data used to train the AI contains biases—whether in terms of gender, race, socioeconomic status, or other factors—the AI is likely to learn and replicate these biases. For example, if a facial recognition system is trained predominantly on images of people from a certain race, it may perform poorly on faces from other races.*

- *Lack of Diversity in Development Teams: Teams that lack diversity in gender, race, culture, or socioeconomic backgrounds might inadvertently overlook potential biases. Diverse teams bring varied perspectives, helping to identify and mitigate biases that others might miss.*

- *Overlooking Contextual and Cultural Nuances: AI developed in one sociocultural context might not translate well to others. For example, language translation AI might struggle with dialects or cultural idioms, leading to misinterpretations.*

- *Inadequate Testing Across Diverse Scenarios: If an AI system is not thoroughly tested across a wide range of scenarios, including diverse datasets, certain biases might remain undetected until the system is deployed.*

- *Simplifying Complex Human Traits: When AI tries to categorize complex human traits or behaviors into overly simplistic or binary groups, it can perpetuate stereotypes and biases. This is often seen in systems that attempt to predict human traits like intelligence, personality, or job suitability.*

- *Feedback Loops: AI systems that continuously learn from user interactions can fall into a feedback loop. If initial biases exist, they can be reinforced over time as the system "learns" from biased user responses or actions.*

- *Lack of Transparency and Explainability: When AI systems are "black boxes" with decision-making processes that are not transparent, identifying and addressing bias becomes challenging. Without clear insights into how decisions are made, it's hard to spot where biases might be creeping in.*

Yes, it's true. Believe it or not, AI can screw up not because it's an evil program but because the people programming it can sometimes be missing a few screws themselves.

And it's not to say every AI fails if the builders are trying to misuse it; clearly, in some of the stories we looked at earlier and the main factors Mira rhymed off, the inappropriate results can be a sheer accident.

This is largely why we're having this conversation. AI ethics are not just for those who have a propensity to abuse technology; they are for everyone that creates, builds, and interacts and is affected by its inputs, outputs, and everything in between. We face a large likelihood of running into a poorly designed AI in the future because companies, individuals, and groups can be misinformed, misusing data, or unaware of what they're unaware of.

And this is why holistic awareness and understanding is so valuable! If you know exactly what's at stake, you can design, build, and use these AI systems in the right ways and avoid being responsible for some truly dismal consequences.

Will: If you were reading this chapter, what would you want yourself to know in order to proactively avoid and correct AI biases?

Mira: If I were a reader delving into this chapter, I would want to be empowered with practical strategies and a mindset focused on proactively addressing AI biases. Here are the key points I would find valuable:

- *Understand the Origins of Bias: Grasping that biases in AI often stem from training data or the perspectives of those who create the systems is crucial. Recognizing that bias is not just a machine problem, but a human issue, sets the foundation for proactive measures.*

- *Diversify Data Sources: Ensure that the data used to train AI systems is as diverse and representative as possible. This includes a wide range of demographics, scenarios, and contexts. It's not just about having large datasets, but about having inclusive datasets.*

- *Foster Diversity in AI Teams: Encourage and support diversity in the teams that are designing, developing, and deploying AI systems. Diverse teams can better identify potential biases and blind spots in AI applications.*

- *Implement Rigorous Testing Protocols: Regularly test AI systems across a variety of scenarios and with diverse user groups. This can help in early identification and correction of biases that might not be immediately obvious.*

- *Establish Ethical Guidelines and Standards: Develop and adhere to ethical guidelines for AI development. This should include principles of fairness, inclusivity, and transparency.*

- *Promote Transparency and Explainability: Strive for AI systems that are as transparent and explainable as possible. Understanding how an AI system arrives at its conclusions is key to identifying and correcting biases.*

- *Engage in Continuous Learning: Recognize that AI, like humans, must continually learn and adapt. Stay informed about the latest developments in AI and ethics, and be prepared to update systems as new understanding emerges.*

- *Community and Stakeholder Engagement: Involve a broad range of stakeholders, including those who might be affected by the AI system, in its development and review. Getting feedback from a wide range of users can provide insights into biases that might not be evident from within the development team.*

- *Legal and Regulatory Compliance: Be aware of and comply with existing laws and regulations related to AI and data usage. As this is an evolving field, staying informed about legal changes is important.*

- *Plan for Accountability: Establish clear protocols for what happens if an AI system does display bias, including how to report it, who is responsible for addressing it, and how to remedy the situation.*

These points illuminate what most consider to be the principles of Responsible AI (RAI):

- Accountability

- Transparency

- Fairness

- Reliability and safety

- Privacy and security

- Inclusiveness

Different organizations may vary in wording and presentation of their concepts, but the principles are the principles.

Here is my go-to guide for understanding how they work and how to practice these pillars: `https://query.prod.cms.rt.microsoft.com/cms/api/am/binary/RE5cmFl`.

In reality, they all come down to the same thing. Whether you are an AI developer, user, architect, decision-maker, or just learning about the tool, can you see the whole picture?

Because, like I mentioned at the start of this chapter, being an ethical ambassador of AI isn't just about having good morals (though, that should definitely be a prerequisite). It's about being aware and considerate of any and all impacts, positive and negative, that your tool may have.

Are you taking the time to collect and manage high-quality data that works to minimize bias?

Do you invite all parties and stakeholders of the system, not just the builders and the overseers to review and understand the thought process of the tool?

Can you do the work to learn, practice, and inform those around you on what exactly goes in to being a responsible user and developer of AI?

There really is a never-ending list of considerations to make when building and using AI tools, but I think the best way to overcome AI bias and the irresponsible use of AI is to just care. And care enough to take action when you see something out of line with the principles and truths of what responsible AI really means.

Will: Thank you, Mira, for these excellent considerations. I think we've put together some great stuff on how the reader can be proactive and aware of AI bias, but obviously, the challenges of using these tools do not end there. Can you put together a little briefing on data privacy and security as this is also a cornerstone of minimizing the negative effects of an AI system?

Mira: Certainly, Will. Data privacy and security are critical pillars in the responsible use of AI. They encompass a range of issues, from how data is collected and stored to how it is used and who has access to it.

Here's a concise briefing on these aspects:

Data Privacy in the AI Context

- *Data Collection: AI systems often require substantial amounts of data to function effectively. However, this data can include sensitive personal information. It's crucial to collect only what's necessary, ensure consent, and be transparent about how data will be used.*

- *Data Storage and Access: Secure storage of data is a fundamental requirement. This involves protecting data from unauthorized access, breaches, and theft. It's essential to have robust security protocols and limit access to sensitive data.*

- *Data Usage: How data is used in AI systems can raise ethical questions. Using personal data for purposes other than what was originally intended or without explicit consent can lead to privacy violations.*

- *Data Sharing: AI often involves sharing data across platforms or with third parties. Ensuring that these entities adhere to privacy standards is crucial.*

Data Security in AI

- *Cybersecurity Measures: AI systems can be targets for cyberattacks. Implementing strong cybersecurity measures to protect AI systems and the data they use is essential.*

- *Vulnerability to Attacks: AI systems, like any technology, have vulnerabilities. Regularly updating and patching these systems to protect against known vulnerabilities is important.*

- *Secure AI Development: Ensuring that AI systems themselves are developed with security in mind can prevent malicious use of AI, like creating deepfakes or exploiting AI systems for personal gain.*

Broader Considerations

- *Regulatory Compliance: Adhering to data protection laws and regulations, such as GDPR in Europe or CCPA in California, is not only legally required but also builds trust with users.*

- *Ethical Considerations: Beyond legal compliance, thinking ethically about how data is used in AI systems is important. This involves considering the impact on individuals and society.*

- *Transparency and Control: Users should have a clear understanding of what data is collected and how it's used. Providing users with control over their data, such as the ability to opt out or access their data, is a key aspect of respecting privacy.*

- *Risk Assessment: Regularly conducting risk assessments to identify potential data privacy and security risks in AI systems can help in proactively addressing these issues.*

As you can see, using AI responsibly isn't just a conversation about how considerate you are when building the models or how effective you are at minimizing bias. AI systems run on data, and that, according to a famous article in *The Economist*, is the new form of currency [3].

Which is the reason it is the target of many nefarious and malicious attacks. When I was first studying RAI, I remember the material I was learning showed a short video about an attack known as data poisoning where hackers manipulate the model training data to corrupt its learning process and therefore skew its outputs [4].

We saw this (in a way) with Microsoft's Twitter chatbot where the users knew the model learned via interaction and therefore "poisoned the water" so to speak.

Thankfully, there are tools that exist in the wonderful world of technology that are specifically designed to help defend AI systems from data privacy and security complications. Here are a few Microsoft ones I've used and found to be quite valuable:

- *Microsoft's FHIR Service in Azure Health Data Service:* This is an Azure service specifically designed for healthcare applications. It has an API call that can be used to anonymize personal health identifying (PHI) data.

- *Microsoft Purview:* A data governance tool for managing access to your organizational data. It uses least-privilege access (`https://learn.microsoft.com/en-us/purview/privileged-access-management`) as well as domain-specific access (sales people have access to sales data but not HR data and vice versa) to ensure the right people of have the right access to the right data.

- *Azure AI Content Safety:* A content moderation platform that uses AI to keep user and AI-generated content safe. It uses advanced language and vision models to accurately detect unsafe or inappropriate content and automatically assign severity scores in real time. It enables your business to review and prioritize flagged items and to take informed action [5].

Will: Thank you, Mira. That does an excellent job of painting the whole picture when it comes to data security and privacy. Now, let's talk about AI and job displacement.

Mira: Certainly, Will. The topic of AI and job displacement is a significant one, marked by both concerns and opportunities. Here's a comprehensive look at this aspect:

Understanding AI-Induced Job Displacement

- *Automation of Repetitive Tasks: AI and automation technologies excel at performing repetitive, routine tasks across various industries. This efficiency can lead to the displacement of jobs that primarily involve such tasks.*

- *Shift in Job Nature: While AI can replace certain tasks, it also creates new job categories and transforms existing ones. Jobs are likely to shift toward roles that require human creativity, problem-solving, emotional intelligence, and interpersonal skills—areas where AI still lags.*

- *Industry-Specific Impacts: The extent of job displacement varies by industry. Sectors with a high degree of routine tasks (like manufacturing or basic data entry) may see more displacement, while others may experience job transformation.*

Roughly once a generation, we have a near panic by some people because technology is destroying jobs. And it's true that new technology often destroys existing jobs, but it also creates many new possibilities through several different channels. Think of cloth making back in the early 19th century or automobile making in the early 20th century. All kinds of supplementary industries, all kinds of new possibilities.

said Richard Cooper, the Maurits C. Boas Professor of International Economics at Harvard University, in a podcast with Peter Gumbel, senior editor at the McKinsey Global Institute, and Susan Land, partner at the McKinsey Global Institute.

To put some numbers on this, we've looked at the productivity growth and employment growth over different time periods in a variety of different countries. And what we find is that since 1960, in the United States, for instance, both productivity and employment have grown in individual years 79 percent of the time. And in only 12 percent of the years did we see productivity growth with employment declines. 95 percent of the time you see productivity and employment growing for all the reasons that Professor Cooper just explained. We see the same pattern in other countries as well. In China, for instance, when you look at individual years, you see employment and productivity both growing in 77 percent of the individual years since 1960. it's very clear from the evidence that, in fact, as productivity grows, you don't see fewer jobs; you see more jobs.—Susan Lund [6]

This discussion supports the underlying message that Mira is trying to illuminate. Which is, really, the fundamental truth when we talk about the effect of emerging technologies like AI on jobs.

Job displacement does not mean the loss of jobs; it means the change of where jobs are. Hence, the displace terminology.

And, more importantly, what those jobs do. In a 2022 article published by the Kellogg School of Management at Northwestern University, researchers found that displacement wasn't just a result of the automation of tasks, but rather than directly replacing workers, technology might change the way their jobs were done and require people to pick up new skills [7].

I think this is the harder reality for most to grasp. As humans, our brains are wired to prioritize a couple of things before anything else: security and the assurance of future security through comfortability.

For the last eon, the mainstream laborer narrative has been built on the idea that you do your job, you learn to do it well, and that's all the learning required to guarantee job stability.

Of course, that's the farthest thing from the truth. The reality is, if it's not technology, there will be another force that disrupts your system of stability and force you to adapt.

One of my favorite stories about this topic comes from my brother; when he first started his job, he had to work a certain number of shifts in the company warehouse as an exercise in getting to know the product and the process of having the product made and shipped to the company's customers. While helping pick orders one day, he was stopped by one of the senior operators and told he should probably slow the pace of his work down.

I can't remember what the reason was that he gave, but the implied reason is obvious: If you are doing my job faster and better than me, I'll be expected to match that level of intensity, and I have no interest in doing that.

I recognize this does not speak for the entire labor force nor does it speak to the character of the operator, but it does help us identify what the problem that, job displacement by emerging technologies like AI, is all about.

The majority of people don't like change.

Naturally, we don't want to adapt unless we must, and that's what technological disruption does—it forces us to adapt whether we like it or not. Which is why the mentality shift needed to embrace job displacement is so simple:

You have to learn to love to learn.

I'll say it one more time since it's kind of a tongue twister:

You have to learn to love to learn!

When I was experiencing rock bottom in my life, the greatest most incredible thing I experienced was that I fell in love with learning again. Because I couldn't coast to good grades anymore, I had to put the work in, study, ask questions, and go to class, and out of that need for adaptation, I acquired the greatest gift I've ever received in life—my undying love for learning.

Learning about the world, about myself, my craft, my role, and impact in society. These are the things that get me out of bed in the morning, and I honestly believe that embracing lifelong learning can do the same for you.

I'm not sure if you're reading this section because you're worried about being displaced or have been displaced, but I want you to know that this could be the best thing that's ever happened to you, that you have an opportunity now to transform not only what you do but who you are and how that looks for you, and that is such a blessing because by embracing change, you become the driver of it.

You want to be the master of your own destiny? Fully accept the reality of never-ending, constantly evolving change, and you can and will transform yourself and your life into whatever you want it to be.

I'm not trying to be esoteric or inspirational, just transparent. I could've failed those courses, sunk deeper into depression, quit school, and gone broke, and no one would be wiser. I could've lived with the regret of not trying for the rest of my life and possibly never tried again because of it. I've seen it happen and I know how real it is.

But you, yes, you reading or listening to this, have to make one, simple choice.

Will you do whatever it takes to become everything you want to become no matter the cost or the bumps along the way?

I know this conversation is about navigating the dark side of AI, but it is just as much about the reflections of these shadows in ourselves, and I hope, if there's anything you take away from this section, this chapter, this book, it's that you are absolutely capable of anything and everything and, with the right tools and using them in the right way, you will make that happen.

Summary: Navigating the Shadows
Introduction

AI holds great potential, but it also presents ethical challenges. This chapter explores the balance between AI innovation and responsibility, highlighting the importance of understanding both its benefits and pitfalls.

Examples of AI Failures

- *ChatGPT Hallucinations:* An attorney used ChatGPT to find case precedents, resulting in fabricated cases and a $5,000 fine.

- *Zillow's Home-Buying Algorithm:* Zillow's algorithm errors led to a failed home-flipping business and a 25% workforce reduction.

- *Healthcare Algorithm Bias:* An algorithm failed to flag high-risk Black patients, highlighting racial biases.

- *Microsoft Chatbot Incident:* A chatbot learned and reproduced racist and misogynistic content from Twitter users.

- *Amazon's Biased Recruitment Tool:* Amazon's AI recruitment tool favored male candidates due to biased training data.

- *Target's Privacy Violation:* Target's analytics revealed a teenager's pregnancy to her family, showcasing privacy concerns.

- These examples demonstrate that AI failures often stem from biased data and human error.

Understanding AI Bias

AI bias occurs when algorithms produce prejudiced outcomes due to flawed data or assumptions. Common causes include:

- *Biased Training Data:* AI learns biases present in the data.

- *Lack of Diversity in Teams:* Homogeneous teams may overlook biases.

- *Oversimplified Human Traits:* Simplifying complex human behaviors can perpetuate stereotypes.

- *Feedback Loops:* Initial biases can be reinforced over time.

- *Lack of Transparency:* Opaque AI systems make bias detection difficult.

Mitigating AI Bias

To proactively avoid and correct AI biases:

- *Diversify Data Sources:* Ensure data is inclusive and representative.

- *Foster Diverse Teams:* Encourage varied perspectives in development teams.

- *Rigorous Testing:* Test AI across diverse scenarios to identify biases.

- *Transparency and Explainability:* Make AI decision processes clear and understandable.

- *Continuous Learning:* Stay informed about AI ethics and developments.

- *Stakeholder Engagement:* Involve diverse stakeholders in AI development.

Principles of Responsible AI

Adopt the following principles for responsible AI (RAI):

- *Accountability:* Ensure clear responsibility for AI outcomes.

- *Transparency:* Make AI operations understandable.

- *Fairness:* Strive for unbiased AI systems.

- *Reliability and Safety:* Ensure AI operates safely.

- *Privacy and Security:* Protect user data.

- *Inclusiveness:* Engage diverse perspectives.

Data Privacy and Security

Data privacy and security are critical for responsible AI use:

- *Data Collection and Usage:* Collect only necessary data and ensure consent.

- *Secure Storage:* Protect data from unauthorized access.

- *Cybersecurity Measures:* Implement strong security protocols.

- *Regulatory Compliance:* Adhere to data protection laws.

AI and Job Displacement

AI can displace jobs, but it also creates new opportunities:

- *Automation of Repetitive Tasks:* AI excels at routine tasks, leading to job displacement in some areas.

- *Shift in Job Nature:* New roles requiring creativity and problem-solving emerge.

- *Continuous Learning:* Embrace lifelong learning to adapt to changing job landscapes.

Conclusion

The chapter emphasizes the importance of ethical considerations in AI development and use. By adopting responsible practices, leveraging diverse data, and fostering continuous learning, businesses can navigate the complexities of AI while minimizing negative impacts. The journey with AI requires a balance of innovation and ethical responsibility to truly harness its potential.

Guardians of Intelligence: Building a Robust AI Governance Framework

I'll be honest; when people started asking me to comment on AI governance, I didn't exactly know what they were talking about. So, I want to start this conversation by defining exactly what I am referring to when I say, "AI governance."

When I say AI governance, I am talking about the principles, policies, and practices that guide the ethical, responsible, and effective implementation of AI technologies within organizations.

To explain it simply, imagine AI as a new team member who needs guidance on how to behave, what tasks to perform, and how to align their actions with the organization's goals.

AI governance is the process of setting up the rules for this "team member," ensuring it works well with humans, protects their interests, and enhances overall performance without overstepping ethical boundaries or making decisions that could harm the organization or society.

As the AI landscape has evolved, the need for robust, human-centered AI governance frameworks has only grown. New technology is great, but when it comes fast and furious with new LLMs, Copilots, and other AI capabilities being released by the big players every other day and having this mixed with ongoing development of regulations and compliance codes like the EU AI Act and Canada's AIDA, having a system for assessing, understanding, utilizing, and deciding on what AI tools to use and how to use them is as imperative as a coffee before a morning standup.

> *Will: Alright Mira, need your help on this one. Can you explain what the purpose of creating an AI governance framework for the reader's organization is? Are there negative consequences to not having one? Are there benefits for creating your own?*
>
> *Mira: Certainly, Will. Here's an explanation that delves into the purpose, consequences of not having an AI governance framework, and the benefits of creating one:*
>
> *Purpose of Creating an AI Governance Framework*
>
> *Ensuring Ethical and Responsible AI Use*
>
> - *Purpose: An AI governance framework helps ensure that AI technologies are used ethically and responsibly within an organization. It establishes guidelines and standards for ethical considerations, including fairness, accountability, transparency, and nondiscrimination.*
>
> - *Negative Consequences: Without a framework, AI systems may inadvertently perpetuate biases, leading to unfair outcomes and potential harm to individuals or groups. This can damage the organization's reputation and lead to legal and regulatory repercussions.*

Compliance with Legal and Regulatory Requirements

- *Purpose: A governance framework ensures compliance with relevant laws and regulations governing AI and data use. It helps organizations stay updated with evolving regulations and avoid legal pitfalls.*

- *Negative Consequences: Noncompliance can result in hefty fines, legal actions, and a loss of trust among stakeholders and customers.*

Risk Management and Mitigation

- *Purpose: Establishing a framework helps identify, assess, and mitigate risks associated with AI deployment, including data privacy breaches, security vulnerabilities, and operational failures.*

- *Negative Consequences: Without a governance structure, organizations may face increased risks of data breaches, cyberattacks, and operational disruptions, leading to financial losses and compromised data integrity.*

Enhancing Transparency and Accountability

- *Purpose: A governance framework promotes transparency and accountability in AI decision-making processes. It ensures that AI systems are explainable and that decision-making processes can be audited and understood by stakeholders.*

- *Negative Consequences: Lack of transparency can lead to mistrust among stakeholders, including customers, employees, and regulators. It can also result in difficulties in diagnosing and correcting errors or biases in AI systems.*

Fostering Innovation and Sustainable Growth

- *Purpose: A well-structured governance framework provides a clear roadmap for AI development and deployment, fostering innovation while ensuring sustainability and scalability. It encourages the responsible exploration of AI's potential.*

- *Negative Consequences: Without a framework, AI initiatives may lack direction and coherence, leading to fragmented efforts, inefficiencies, and missed opportunities for innovation.*

Benefits of Creating Your Own AI Governance Framework

Tailored to Organizational Needs

- *Benefit: Developing a custom governance framework allows organizations to address their specific needs, objectives, and operational contexts. It ensures that the framework aligns with the organization's values and strategic goals.*

- *Example: Custom frameworks can incorporate industry-specific regulations and best practices, ensuring relevance and effectiveness.*

Enhanced Organizational Culture

- *Benefit: A governance framework fosters a culture of responsibility and ethical awareness within the organization. It encourages employees to adhere to best practices and to be vigilant about ethical considerations in AI development.*

- *Example: Training programs and ethical guidelines
  integrated into the framework can raise awareness
  and improve adherence to ethical standards across the
  organization.*

Improved Stakeholder Trust

- *Benefit: A robust governance framework enhances trust
  among stakeholders, including customers, investors,
  and regulatory bodies. Demonstrating a commitment
  to ethical AI practices can strengthen relationships and
  reputation.*

- *Example: Transparent reporting and regular audits
  as part of the governance framework can provide
  assurance to stakeholders about the integrity and
  reliability of AI systems.*

Proactive Risk Management

- *Benefit: Custom frameworks enable proactive
  identification and mitigation of risks specific to the
  organization's AI applications. This ensures that
  potential issues are addressed before they escalate.*

- *Example: Regular risk assessments and contingency
  planning can be built into the framework to handle
  unforeseen challenges effectively.*

Long-Term Strategic Advantage

- *Benefit: A well-defined governance framework provides
  a strategic advantage by enabling the organization to
  adapt to future regulatory changes and technological
  advancements seamlessly.*

- *Example: Organizations with established governance
  structures can quickly adjust their policies and
  practices in response to new regulations or emerging
  AI technologies, maintaining compliance and
  competitiveness.*

*In summary, creating an AI governance framework is essen-
tial for ensuring ethical, transparent, and secure AI practices
within an organization. It mitigates risks, enhances stakeholder trust, and fosters a culture of responsibility and innovation. Without such a framework, organizations face
significant ethical, legal, and operational risks that can under-
mine their success and sustainability.*

Now I know we've already delved into responsible AI and talked about
data privacy and security as well as AI strategy in business, but the focus of
this chapter is on something a little less, explicit.

An analogy that comes to mind is that AI governance is like table
manners. Each house interprets what these manners look like, why they
are in place, and who's responsible for abiding them a little bit differently.
In contrast, responsible AI is more of the objective laws like having smoke
alarms on each floor of the house. They are the safeguards that are not
up for interpretation and, at the end of the day, legally required to ensure
compliance and safety.

This is what makes AI governance an enigmatic subject to explore;
there's no real definition or objective standard. Though I've defined the
term above, this is simply my interpretation, and you should feel inclined
to define the structure and practice that fits you and your organization's
goals and principles for AI the best!

That being said, I do want to spend the rest of this chapter explicitly
outlining what I've seen work and not work when it comes to creating
these frameworks and what methodologies I would consider exploring if I
were in your shoes.

The Fundamentals

Data Loss Prevention (DLP) Policies

A great AI governance framework should really piggyback on your data governance framework.

Note   If you're not sure what or if your organization has a data governance framework, I suggest you put this book down and figure that out first. Facetiousness aside, you will not be able to effectively implement any of the following suggestions if you don't have an existing data governance framework.

Which is why I started with DLP policies; DLP policies are essentially a set of strategies and tools designed to ensure that sensitive information does not get lost, misused, or accessed by unauthorized users. It acts as a comprehensive security framework that monitors and controls data flow and access within and outside your organization.

An AI does not inherently know the difference between personal, public, general, confidential, and highly confidential data. It also does not know what data is outdated or garbage data. Your DLP policies are how you explain to the AI what these characteristics are and how to interpret them.

DLP policies are not limited to just teaching your AI how to use your data so there's no controversial leaks. It's actually much more about maintaining trust and integrity within your data management processes.

For example, imagine your tasked with creating a new company intranet. The sites on the intranet must house all company documentation, news, policies, procedures, and practically anything anyone in the company would need access to.

But you can't give everyone access to everything; I mean you could, but your likelihood for job security would probably torpedo.

117

Wouldn't it be amazing if there was a manual that outlined who had access to what and whether that was based on their role, their team, or some other privilege?

That's the importance of your DLP policies in a nutshell; they are the governing body for all data access and movement which is vital for much more than how smart your AI is.

Of course, there are some additional characteristics of DLP policies that are particularly useful in an AI governance framework.

Data Breaching

AI initiatives often involve large datasets that include sensitive and proprietary information.

Without DLP policies, there is a high risk of data breaches during the development and testing phases. DLP ensures that all data used in AI projects is protected from unauthorized access and misuse.

Compliance

AI projects frequently handle vast amounts of personal and sensitive data, which must comply with regulations such as GDPR, HIPAA, and CCPA. DLP policies ensure that your AI initiatives adhere to these regulations, avoiding legal complications and fines.

Quality Assurance

The success of AI models depends on the quality and integrity of the data they are trained on.

DLP policies help maintain this integrity by preventing data corruption and unauthorized modifications.

Key Takeaways

- Ensure that your DLP policies cover all possible data exit points, including email, cloud storage, endpoints, and removable media.

- Train your team on the importance of data security and the specifics of your DLP policies. Awareness programs help prevent accidental data leaks and ensure that everyone involved in the AI project understands their role in protecting sensitive information.

- Your DLP solutions should seamlessly integrate with the tools and platforms used in AI development. This ensures that data protection measures are in place throughout the entire AI lifecycle, from data collection to model deployment.

- As your AI initiatives grow, your DLP policies should scale accordingly.

Explainable AI (XAI): The Methodology for Building Confidence in Your AI Systems
XAI refers to a set of techniques and approaches designed to make the decision-making processes of AI systems more transparent and understandable to humans.

It bridges the gap between the "black box" nature of AI algorithms and the need for users to trust, interpret, and validate AI-generated outcomes [2]. A comparison of a traditional and XAI workflow is shown in Figure 7-1.

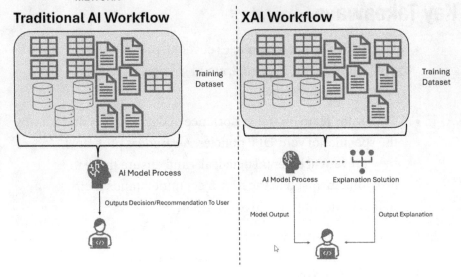

Figure 7-1. *A simple comparison of a traditional and XAI workflow; the AI Model Process represents the trained AI model and its output to the user. The Explanation Solution represents the method, algorithm, etc. applied to the AI model and its output to create a human-digestible explanation of the model output and thought process*

Think of XAI as your way of making the AI model "show its work." You design and implement systems that effectively share the AI's thought process, what data it considered when responding, and why. Basically, how and why it reached the conclusion it did.

Why Does XAI Matter for Businesses?

- *Trust and Accountability:* Transparent AI decisions build trust with users, customers, and regulators. When people understand how AI arrives at conclusions, they are more likely to accept and rely on those decisions.

- *Legal and Ethical Compliance:* Regulatory bodies increasingly demand transparency in AI systems. XAI helps businesses comply with regulations by providing clear explanations for AI-driven choices.

- *Risk Mitigation:* Understanding AI decisions allows businesses to identify errors, biases, or unintended consequences. This enables timely corrections and reduces risk.

- *Business Growth:* Organizations that establish digital trust through practices like XAI are more likely to experience revenue and EBIT growth [3].

It's about maximizing the benefit of the new technology while acknowledging and respecting the risks involved. Knowing how models derive conclusions and being able to explain their thought process and what data they use produces trust in their results.

Without this understanding of "what's happening under the hood" of your AI model, establishing digital trust with consumers of AI products or with employees using AI tools is an uphill battle.

Techniques and Tools for XAI

- *Feature Importance:* Create a system that breaks down which variables (features) contribute most to the AI model's outputs. For example, does the model base its response to the user on location information? Does it rely on specific user information like permissions, company role, etc.?

- *Local Explanations:* Explain the cause-and-effect relationship of inputs and AI model outputs by isolating variables for a specific interaction. For example, say you have a junior and senior analyst using an AI insight tool. Do they receive the same output?

Is there censored data that only the senior analyst can see? Focus on why the AI is designed to return the output it returns so you can identify these major factors and find their relationships to the model output.

- *Visualizations:* Everything's better with a visual! Create an interpretable visual representation of model behavior. For example, if you are using an LLM in a RAG application, you could create a graph that displays the number of times the LLM referenced a particular document, what excerpts it used for each interaction, and how the user rated the quality of the response based on these characteristics.

- *Rule-Based Systems:* Develop rules that guide AI decisions, making them more transparent. For example, if you are using a CNN to identify whether someone has access to a building, you might have an algorithm that is run first to check if the user is wearing glasses and if they are, asks the user to remove them to ensure a higher accuracy when making the access scan. Rule-based systems are controls you should design to simplify the buildup to or follow up steps after the execution of the AI module in your system to easily understand the decision path of the model.

- *LIME (Local Interpretable Model-Agnostic Explanations):* This is essentially an algorithm for automating local explanations. It is a model that provides interpretable explanations for individual predictions made by any machine learning model. It is an AI that simplifies the output of a more complex AI to understand its decision process. Kind of cool or weird, whatever you prefer!

- *SHAP (Shapley Additive Explanations):* An algorithm
  that automates feature importance mathematically.
  Another AI helping AI situation, so cool or weird!

AI Information vs. AI Influence

One of the key elements of enacting an AI governance framework is creating a decision framework for acting and investing in the right tools and products. Larger companies are dropping six figures into AI projects without hesitation, and, according to Cognizant, the average ROI is only 1.3%. Further, with potentially high upfront costs in data modernization, technology adoption, and people development, it can take 17 months on average to realize positive payback [4].

This is probably slightly deflating, I know, but this does not have to be your company's story. Having a methodology for strategically acquiring AI software or investing in internal initiatives can dramatically alter these results.

As a kid, I played a popular game called *Pokemon.* At the start of every *Pokemon* game, you have to select what's called your "starter" *Pokemon.* This is the first *Pokemon* you own in the game.

The reason I mention this is because that starter *Pokemon* is basically your main asset throughout the entirety of the game. You, of course, can acquire and invest in other *Pokemon* and eventually not need your starter, but nonetheless, you only get one starter.

This manifests in a similar fashion on a company's AI development journey. The initial tech stack, software, tools, and models you choose are not permanent, but they are undoubtedly a foundation that's difficult to move forward without.

This is why a decision framework is critical. Knowing how to decide on what assets to acquire and invest in to kickstart and grow your company's AI innovation is a skill needed to be successful in this space.

So, what is the key to this framework? To me, it's developing the understanding of the difference between AI information and AI influence.

AI information manifests as factual data, research findings, and unbiased insights about AI technologies, their capabilities, and limitations. For example, technical papers, empirical studies, and expert analyses fall into this category.

AI influence involves opinions, popular trends, speculative predictions, and hype surrounding AI. It could be the sensational portrayal of AI in media, the exaggerated claims of AI startups, or the fearmongering about AI taking over jobs.

Having a dedicated process for discerning these differences helps you acquire and invest in the right AI technologies without becoming disoriented by the sheer mass and intensity of the AI rumor mill.

AI Red Teaming

The reality of AI innovation is that, for every advent like GPT 4 or DALL-E, there are **very** smart people out there that use these tools to hack, scam, and manipulate systems and people into disclosing confidential information, transferring funds, and performing other nefarious acts that harm people and systems.

We've all seen a headline or two about AI being used to deep fake some authority or algorithms that penetrate security systems to make a ruckus, and your AI governance framework must have the controls and redundancies in place to protect against these possibilities.

I'll always remember, on one of my first AI projects, we were ready to deploy the pilot solution, and the client insisted we take every security precaution possible before deploying because, in Germany, sites are constantly being attacked by bots.

Sure enough, within minutes of deployment, the site had already been attacked a handful of times. Of course, the systems we set up to protect the LLM and data held up, but it was eye-opening to see just how intense the security landscape can be. Especially now that bad actors are armed with the same capabilities as the rest of us.

Don't be alarmed; this is why we're covering AI red teaming. Red teaming is the process of simulating attacks on your own system in order to uncover hidden vulnerabilities and address them before they become real threats. It might seem a little unorthodox to try and break your own beautiful system you just built, but it is a necessary evil because if you don't, someone else will.

Will: Mira, can you provide the reader with a couple of techniques on how to start incorporating AI red teaming into their AI governance framework, please?

Mira: Absolutely, Will. Here are a couple of techniques to help readers start incorporating AI red teaming into their AI governance framework:

- *Establish a Dedicated AI Red Team*

    - *Objective: Form a team of experts whose primary responsibility is to identify, challenge, and mitigate potential risks and vulnerabilities in AI systems.*

    - *Composition: Include diverse members with expertise in AI, cybersecurity, ethics, and domain-specific knowledge to ensure a comprehensive approach.*

    - *Tasks*

        - *Threat Modeling: Conduct threat modeling sessions to identify potential attack vectors and vulnerabilities specific to your AI systems.*

        - *Simulated Attacks: Perform simulated attacks on AI models to test their resilience against adversarial inputs, data poisoning, and other threats.*

        - *Regular Audits: Schedule regular audits and assessments to ensure continuous monitoring and improvement of AI security measures.*

- *Implement Continuous Monitoring and Feedback Loops*

    - *Objective: Establish continuous monitoring and feedback mechanisms to detect and respond to vulnerabilities and ethical concerns in real time.*

    - *Techniques*

        - *Anomaly Detection: Use AI and machine learning tools to monitor AI systems for unusual behavior or anomalies that could indicate security breaches or ethical issues.*

        - *Feedback Integration: Create channels for stakeholders, including employees and customers, to report any suspicious activities or concerns related to AI systems. Ensure this feedback is promptly reviewed and acted upon by the AI red team.*

        - *Performance Metrics: Track performance metrics and key indicators related to AI system behavior, fairness, and compliance. Use these metrics to identify areas requiring red teaming focus.*

- *Develop Comprehensive Training Programs*

    - *Objective: Equip your AI red team and broader organization with the necessary skills and knowledge to effectively manage AI risks.*

    - *Components:*

        - *Ethical Training: Provide training on ethical AI use, focusing on bias mitigation, fairness, and transparency. Ensure all team members understand the ethical implications of AI systems.*

- *Security Awareness: Conduct regular workshops and simulations to keep the AI red team and other stakeholders updated on the latest AI security threats and mitigation strategies.*

- *Collaboration and Sharing: Encourage collaboration and knowledge-sharing among different departments and teams. Foster a culture of continuous learning and improvement.*

- *Incorporate AI Red Teaming into the Development Lifecycle:*

  - *Objective: Integrate AI red teaming activities into each stage of the AI development lifecycle to proactively address risks.*

  - *Stages*

    - *Design Phase: Involve the AI red team in the design phase to identify potential vulnerabilities and ethical concerns early on. Use threat modeling and scenario analysis to anticipate risks.*

    - *Development Phase: During development, conduct regular code reviews, security assessments, and adversarial testing. Ensure that the AI red team provides continuous feedback to the development team.*

    - *Deployment and Post-Deployment: After deployment, implement robust monitoring and incident response mechanisms. Regularly update and refine AI models based on insights gained from red teaming activities.*

*By incorporating these techniques into their AI governance
framework, organizations can enhance the security, fairness,
and reliability of their AI systems. AI red teaming helps proactively identify and mitigate risks, ensuring that AI technologies are used responsibly and ethically.*

I know, there are a lot of things to consider in an AI governance
framework, and I'm sure it feels like if any one of these are missed, it could
all end in disaster. But that's kind of the point, there are endless things you
can do in an AI governance framework; some will be vital for your projects,
others will be irrelevant and can be ignored.

The only way to find what works is to try and find what works. Try one
of these components, assess its impact on your framework, evaluate where
to go next, rinse, and repeat.

Remember, lessons and momentum drive success in any AI endeavor,
and you have to iterate on this framework to achieve something that works
best for your organization and customer base.

As a closing thought, I would recommend starting with your company's
principles. What is your approach to serving your customers? How do you
support employees? What are the overarching guardrails that guide the
efficacy and efficiency of the rest of your business operations, and how
does this apply to managing your firm's AI innovation?

The term governance derives from the Greek verb *kubernaein*
(*kubernáo*), meaning to steer; so look at your AI governance framework
as an opportunity to align technological innovation with your company's
direction and blaze a path forward to a future where you make the most of
what AI has to offer.

Summary: Building a Robust AI Governance Framework

Introduction to AI Governance

AI governance refers to the principles, policies, and practices that guide the ethical, responsible, and effective implementation of AI technologies within organizations. It ensures that AI systems align with organizational goals, protect human interests, and operate within ethical boundaries.

Purpose and Importance of AI Governance

1. *Ensuring Ethical and Responsible AI Use*

   - *Purpose:* Establish guidelines for fairness, accountability, transparency, and nondiscrimination.

   - *Consequences:* Without it, AI systems can perpetuate biases, harm individuals, and damage reputations.

2. *Compliance with Legal and Regulatory Requirements*

   - *Purpose:* Stay updated with laws and avoid legal issues.

   - *Consequences:* Noncompliance can result in fines and loss of trust.

3. *Risk Management and Mitigation*

   - *Purpose:* Identify and mitigate risks such as data breaches and operational failures.

   - *Consequences:* Increased risks of data breaches and financial losses.

4. *Enhancing Transparency and Accountability*

- *Purpose:* Ensure AI decision-making processes are explainable and auditable.

- *Consequences:* Lack of transparency leads to mistrust and difficulty in correcting errors.

5. *Fostering Innovation and Sustainable Growth*

- *Purpose:* Provide a clear roadmap for AI development, fostering innovation.

- *Consequences:* Without it, efforts may be fragmented and inefficient.

Benefits of Creating Your Own AI Governance Framework

1. *Tailored to Organizational Needs*

- *Benefit:* Address specific needs and align with strategic goals.

- *Example:* Industry-specific regulations and best practices.

2. *Enhanced Organizational Culture*

- *Benefit:* Foster a culture of responsibility and ethical awareness.

- *Example:* Training programs and ethical guidelines.

3. *Improved Stakeholder Trust*

- *Benefit:* Strengthen relationships and reputation.

- *Example:* Transparent reporting and regular audits.

4. *Proactive Risk Management*

- *Benefit:* Address potential issues before they escalate.

- *Example:* Regular risk assessments and contingency planning.

5. *Long-Term Strategic Advantage*

- *Benefit:* Adapt to regulatory changes and technological advancements.

- *Example:* Quickly adjust policies and practices to maintain compliance and competitiveness.

Key Components of AI Governance Framework

1. *Data Loss Prevention (DLP) Policies*

- *Importance:* Protect sensitive information and maintain data integrity.

- *Key Takeaways:* Ensure policies cover all data exit points and integrate with AI development tools.

2. *Explainable AI (XAI)*

- *Importance:* Build trust and accountability by making AI decision processes transparent.

- *Techniques:* Feature importance, local explanations, visualizations, rule-based systems, LIME, and SHAP.

3. *AI Information vs. AI Influence*

    - *Concept:* Differentiate factual AI data from hype
      and trends.

    - *Benefit:* Make informed decisions on AI
      technologies and investments.

4. *AI Red Teaming*

    - *Purpose:* Simulate attacks to uncover
      vulnerabilities.

    - *Techniques:* Establish a dedicated AI red team,
      continuous monitoring, comprehensive training,
      and integration into the development lifecycle.

Conclusion

Creating an AI governance framework is essential for managing AI
technologies ethically and effectively. It involves establishing clear
principles, policies, and practices tailored to organizational needs. By
focusing on data protection, transparency, informed decision-making, and
proactive risk management, organizations can harness AI's potential while
mitigating its risks. The journey toward robust AI governance is iterative,
requiring continuous evaluation and adaptation to align with evolving
technological and regulatory landscapes.

CHAPTER 8

Charting the Course: Equipping Your Knowledge and Skills for the AI Horizon

Without question, we're in the new age of technology. Outside of the groundbreaking advents of the last couple of years, there's a more important shift in how people are approaching the world's problems with AI as the catalyst for their solutions.

I can't even count the number of times myself or someone I've been speaking with has said, "Use ChatGPT for that..." or "Let AI figure it out..." because we've reached a point in society where there is a common understanding that AI has real-world utility. We're of course nowhere close to any sort of iRobot dystopia, but the level of acceptance and embracement for AI as an overall concept is growing rapidly.

Though this is pretty fantastic, there's one critical consideration that we've all got to make as we prepare to enter the AI renaissance:

We have to grow into people that can use AI adequately.

© The Editor(s) (if applicable) and The Author(s),
under exclusive license to APress Media, LLC, part of Springer Nature 2024
W. Hawkins, *AI Essentials Guide*, https://doi.org/10.1007/979-8-8688-0911-8_8

Most of us grew up with AI being science fiction—a reality that only existed in our imaginations or George Lucas' notebook. We tend to create false expectations on exactly what level of technological innovation is possible over our lifetime.

This belief derives from a well-known concept known as Moore's law which essentially discovered the premise for the idea that technological advancements tend to accelerate exponentially over time. What took 50 years to invent in 1960 would be passed by something more advanced in five years today [1].

The reason I share this is because AI is not really one invention; it's a paradigm shift. The smartphone may have been brought to the world by Apple, but its effect on how people interact with each other, with the world, with businesses, with schools, with everything has changed forever. Twenty years ago, it would be an absurd waste of time to build a mobile-friendly website, and today, it is an unspoken requirement for any website stood up.

This is the same paradigm shift we're experiencing with AI, only stronger and faster. We're already encountering fully automated chatbots and self-driving cars; soon, there will be intelligent T-shirts, pets, and probably an AI Olympics.

I know this seems scary but it's actually pretty amazing. As we've discussed on multiple occasions, AI becoming a part of our day-to-day activities is as needed as it is scary; we're at a state in society where intelligent applications, data-driven tools, and digital assistants are not just savvy, they're essential.

Which means we need to raise our level of awareness, understanding, and skills to be able to truly benefit from all of these life-changing innovations.

This chapter will help you see how to cultivate the essential skills, harness the power of community, and turn the challenge of an AI-driven future into your greatest adventure.

At this point in the story, my hope is that you've not only gained a new outlook on AI but see the change it is enacting in the world as a catalyst for you to change whatever you'd like to change about your situation both personally and professionally.

If not, well, this chapter should at least equip you with some idea of how to create a skillset that will set you up for success in this new, AI-driven reality.

Will: Mira, with so many new and different AI tools coming out every day and the accelerated innovation of models and AI architectures, what would you say the reader should focus on the most in order to educate and upskill themselves in a way that they are ready to embrace the AI-driven future with tenacity?

Mira: That's an important question, Will. In an environment of rapidly evolving AI technologies, focusing on foundational skills and adaptable learning strategies is key. Here's what readers should consider:

1. *Understand the Basics of AI and Machine Learning: Start with a solid understanding of the fundamentals. This includes knowing how AI and machine learning work, basic concepts like algorithms, neural networks, and data processing. This foundational knowledge will remain relevant despite changes in tools and technologies.*

2. *Data Literacy: Since AI heavily relies on data, understanding how to analyze, interpret, and use data is crucial. This doesn't necessarily mean becoming a data scientist but having a good grasp of data's role and how it informs AI decisions.*

3. *Problem-Solving Skills: AI is ultimately a tool for solving problems. Fostering strong analytical and problem-solving skills will enable readers to effectively apply AI solutions, regardless of the specific technology or model.*

4. *Coding and Technical Skills: While not everyone needs to be an expert coder, basic programming knowledge, particularly in languages commonly used in AI like Python, can be extremely beneficial.*

5. *Ethical and Societal Implications: Understanding the ethical dimensions and societal impacts of AI is increasingly important. This includes topics like bias in AI, privacy concerns, and the ethical use of AI technologies.*

6. *Continuous Learning Mindset: Perhaps the most important skill is the ability to continuously learn and adapt. AI and technology fields evolve rapidly, so staying curious, engaged, and willing to learn new things is vital.*

7. *Soft Skills: Skills like creativity, emotional intelligence, communication, and collaboration are critical. As AI takes over more technical or repetitive tasks, these uniquely human skills become even more valuable.*

8. *Industry-Specific Knowledge: Depending on one's field, understanding how AI is being applied in that industry can provide a significant advantage. Whether it's AI in healthcare, finance, education, or another sector, industry-specific knowledge will help in leveraging AI effectively.*

Mira makes some great points here, but I want to focus on a couple of key notions:

1. *Mastering the Fundamentals*

    There's really nothing more important than this in any discipline. While I was in my fourth year of university, I had the honor of working and studying with a brilliant econometrician and data scientist who, in my humble opinion, is the smartest human I know and more importantly one of the most disciplined.

    On the odd occasion of me showing up to the class we were both taking at that time, I'd always find him rigorously studying and applying the material we were learning, even if it was stuff we had learned earlier in our university careers. He used to say, "You are never too good to practice the fundamentals," and I honestly can't think of a more important statement when it comes to working with emerging technologies like AI.

    Even with the insane pace of model development experienced in the last year and surely what we will continue to see for years to come, the fundamentals of machine learning continue to remain at play.

    A large language model is nothing more than a massive neural network with billions of data points, and any image analyzer or creator is also some insanely sophisticated neural network.

    The reality of AI is this:

No matter how the model interacts with you on the outside, at the foundational level, it still functions the same on the inside.

All AI models are powered by data and run on compute; the rest is purely an expression of how the end user wants to experience the outcome the model is designed to produce.

That's why taking the time to learn the conceptual process of data going in and out of any machine learning model whether it is an LLM, a GAN, a CNN, or an RNN is critical. Knowing how you can use the data to get from input to output will dictate your ability to leverage the tools that are in demand.

2. *Working Out Your "Problem-Solving" Muscles*

In any circumstance that AI is involved, whether it be a personal productivity device, an enterprise project, or just you screwing around, your ability to handle barriers, obstacles, and any unforeseen stipulations will be what makes the difference not just with your AI skillset but any skillset you pursue in life. What makes these muscles especially important in the context of AI and machine learning is that using and building AI tools is almost always an **iterative process**.

Think about your use of ChatGPT or M365 Copilot. When you use these tools to solve a real-world problem you're working on, it is very rare that they give you the exact information you need to solve the problem outright. There is usually a

138

period of figuring out how to describe the problem and then identifying the important context and considerations that surround the problem and its solution. This is usually followed by a period of trial and error of some kind, and it can really take a fair amount of effort, patience, and persistence to get to the solution you want and/or need.

This process I'm describing is the real skillset of being ready for an AI-driven future. Every prompt you write and completion you receive is largely based on your ability to understand the problem you face and identify how the solution should be characterized.

As we've discussed in previous parts of the text, there are two ingredients to being successful with AI in any case: a feedback loop and momentum, and an individual's ability to problem-solve is really the catalyst for these two vital components.

3. *Coding and Technical Skills*

Though I agree with Mira, basic programming knowledge can be extremely beneficial especially in the context of more complex AI systems, I don't think any programming knowledge is required to be successful in the age of AI.

There has been a quiet revolution in the world of software development in the last few years. Low-/no-code platforms and software have been popping up all over the technology landscape and can really bolster the practical capabilities of anyone that can click a mouse and type in a text box.

The Microsoft Power Platform is a great example of a proficient low-/ no-code platform for developing business and AI-powered business applications without needing to hire a team of software developers or AI engineers.

Now, do I think this platform and others like it replace the incredible value of developers? Of course not; they are great tools for basic use cases and scenarios but are not the best-equipped for advanced applications and complex scenarios.

But, that's really the point of the low-/no-code revolution. Not every AI or business application use case warrants an incredibly complex design and codebase. These low-code tools not only help people who do not come from a computer science background; they also:

- Lower the barrier to entry for businesses trying to take advantage of AI

- Offer streamlined interoperability so that connecting data to an AI model and connecting the AI model to the end user is efficient and accelerated

- Turbo-charge the iterative process of using and building AI because not as much time is spent in development so you can accelerate prototyping and therefore get feedback faster and more often

What I'm trying to say is, before you go spend a bunch of time and money on a Python coding bootcamp, spend some time exploring and building AI using low-/no-code tools like the Power Platform or Azure Machine Learning Designer to really get an understanding of where your skill gaps truly lie.

If you're struggling to build a model because of syntax issues, you're probably not using the best tool for your skillset. If you can't figure out how to build the model even though you have the data you want, maybe you need to spend some more time working on the fundamentals.

Will: Those are great points, Mira. For the people reading this book who want to invest in AI education and upskilling, who are some credible sources they can follow and what are some good courses or training programs that would be a great place for them to get started on building their hands-on technology skills?

Mira: That's a great follow-up, Will. For readers looking to delve into AI education and upskilling, there are several reputable sources and courses to consider. Here's a curated list to get started:

Credible Sources to Follow

- *Coursera: Offers courses in partnership with top universities and organizations. Courses range from introductory to advanced levels in AI and machine learning.*

- *edX: Similar to Coursera, edX provides a range of AI-related courses from respected institutions.*

- *Udacity: Known for its nanodegree programs, Udacity offers specialized courses in AI, machine learning, and data science.*

- *Fast.ai: Offers practical and cutting-edge courses in deep learning, emphasizing hands-on learning.*

- *DeepLearning.AI: Founded by Andrew Ng, this is an excellent resource for deep learning specialization.*

- *Kaggle: Besides hosting AI and data science competitions, Kaggle offers microcourses that cover specific AI skills and tools.*

- *MIT OpenCourseWare: Provides free access to course content from MIT, including AI and computer science.*

- *Google AI: Offers a range of resources, including tutorials and research papers, great for staying updated with the latest in AI.*

Recommended Courses and Programs

- *Machine Learning by Andrew Ng (Coursera): A highly recommended introductory course in machine learning.*

- *AI for Everyone by Andrew Ng (Coursera): Ideal for nontechnical individuals, offering a broad overview of AI.*

- *Deep Learning Specialization (Coursera): A series of comprehensive courses for those interested in deep learning.*

- *Introduction to Artificial Intelligence (edX): Provided by IBM, this course covers the basics of AI.*

- *AI Programming with Python Nanodegree (Udacity): A good starting point for programming in AI.*

- *AI for Business Leaders (Udacity): Tailored for business professionals to understand and apply AI strategically.*

- *Practical Deep Learning for Coders (Fast.ai): A hands-on approach to deep learning.*

- *TensorFlow Developer Certificate Program (Coursera): Focuses on using TensorFlow, a popular tool in AI and machine learning.*

Hands-On Technology Skills

- *Python Programming: Widely used in AI; start with basic Python and then move to libraries like TensorFlow and PyTorch.*

- *Data Science and Analysis: Fundamental skills in data handling and analysis are crucial.*

- *SQL and data visualization tools like Tableau can also be valuable.*

- *Deep Learning and Neural Networks: Focus on understanding the architecture of neural networks and how to implement them.*

Personally, I've really enjoyed the educational resources offered by Andrew Ng; he is one of the godfathers of modern machine learning, so if you're looking for someone to provide guidance on what and how to get the right information for leveraging AI in your situation, his LinkedIn or website are probably some of the best places to go.

Mira mentioned a couple of good certification programs, but I would also suggest looking at the professional certification programs offered by industry giants like Amazon, Google, and Microsoft. These are not only great holistic training opportunities, but they also give you hands-on experience with industry-favored tools and platforms like AWS or Azure and offer assets for those looking to advance or transition on their career path. The AI-900 certification offered by Microsoft is a great example because it not only teaches you the fundamentals of AI; it also walks you through how to develop some basic solutions using Azure services like Computer Vision and Cognitive Services.

The other key in being prepared for the AI horizon is getting others involved in your learning and/or upskilling journey. In university, I learned very quickly that training, studying, and learning alone is 10× harder than doing it in parallel with others. When you train with others, you can escape your own interpretation of the material and benefit from another pair of eyes looking at the same subject, and there's really nothing more valuable than that.

Of course, there's also the age-old maxim that you don't really know something until you can teach it to others, and collaborating and sharing learnings with a community can absolutely provide this opportunity for your development path.

> *Will: Mira, as you know, the other massively important factor in being prepared for the AI horizon is having readers share and collaborate on AI projects or initiatives and participate in AI communities. Can you make some suggestions on how people should go about involving other people or communities in their learning journey?*

> *Mira: Absolutely, Will. Collaboration and community involvement are crucial in the AI journey, as they bring diverse perspectives, foster innovation, and offer support. Here are some ways readers can involve others and engage with AI communities:*

> *Joining AI Communities and Forums*

> - *Online Forums and Social Media: Platforms like Reddit (subreddits like r/MachineLearning, r/artificial), LinkedIn groups, and Twitter (following AI experts and hashtags) are great for discussions and staying updated.*

> - *GitHub: Participating in open source AI projects on GitHub can provide practical experience and community interaction.*

- *Meetup and Eventbrite: Look for local or virtual AI meetups, workshops, and seminars. These can be found on platforms like Meetup.com or Eventbrite.*

- *Professional Networks: Join professional organizations like the Association for the Advancement of Artificial Intelligence (AAAI) or IEEE Computer Society.*

Collaborating on AI Projects

- *Hackathons and Competitions: Participate in AI hackathons or competitions like those on Kaggle. These events are excellent for learning, networking, and showcasing skills.*

- *Collaborative Projects: Seek opportunities to collaborate on projects through platforms like GitHub or even in local community groups or universities.*

- *Study Groups: Form or join study groups with peers. Platforms like Discord or Slack can facilitate virtual group learning and project collaboration.*

Engaging in AI Initiatives

- *Contribute to Open Source: Contributing to open source AI projects can help improve skills, understand real-world applications, and connect with other enthusiasts and professionals.*

- *Attend Conferences and Workshops: Participating in AI conferences (like NeurIPS, ICML, or local tech conferences) can be enlightening and provide networking opportunities.*

- *Online Webinars and Workshops: Many organizations and universities offer free or paid webinars and workshops. These can be excellent opportunities for learning and meeting like-minded individuals.*

Building a Learning Network

- *Mentorship: Seek mentors in the AI field or offer to mentor others. Platforms like LinkedIn can be useful for connecting with potential mentors or mentees.*

- *Blogging and Content Creation: Sharing your learning journey through blogging or creating content on platforms like Medium, YouTube, or a personal blog can attract a community and encourage exchanges of ideas.*

- *Collaborative Learning Platforms: Engage in platforms like Coursera, edX, or Udacity, which often have forums or groups for discussion and collaboration.*

By actively engaging in these communities and collaborative efforts, readers can not only enhance their own understanding and skills in AI but also contribute to the broader AI ecosystem. Collaboration in AI is a two-way street—it's about both learning from the community and contributing back to it.

I have some other communities and forums that I am a part of that I will include in the appendix for those looking for more groups to participate in.

As you can see, advancing your own personal or organizational understanding of the AI revolution is not a simple endeavor, which is why it is so important to start right now.

No, I don't mean tomorrow or next week, I mean right this second. You've been doing great so far at listening to my rambling, and I greatly appreciate that but that doesn't get you off the hook!

I will end this chapter here because I want you to take the next five mins to either sign up for a course, download an ebook, or join an AI community (of course, choose a credible one).

Do something today that will help you tomorrow. As I've mentioned countless times now, an AI journey is an ITERATIVE process driven by feedback and momentum, so this is not up for debate.

Drop whatever you're doing right now, and find something to do that will continue your learning journey. If you don't, you will continue to feel overwhelmed and anxious about what's to come.

Summary: Equipping Your Knowledge and Skills for the AI Horizon

Introduction

We are in the midst of a new age of technology, with AI emerging as a significant catalyst for solving the world's problems. As AI becomes more integrated into daily life, it is essential to develop the skills and knowledge necessary to leverage this technology effectively.

The Importance of Growing with AI

- *Technological Acceptance:* AI has moved from science fiction to a practical tool in various aspects of life.

- *Paradigm Shift:* AI represents a fundamental change similar to the advent of the smartphone, impacting how we interact with technology and each other.

Key Skills for the AI-Driven Future

1. *Understanding AI and Machine Learning Basics:* Grasp the fundamental concepts of AI, including algorithms, neural networks, and data processing.

2. *Data Literacy:* Develop the ability to analyze, interpret, and use data effectively.

3. *Problem-Solving Skills:* Enhance analytical and problem-solving abilities to apply AI solutions effectively.

4. *Coding and Technical Skills:* Basic programming knowledge, especially in languages like Python, can be beneficial.

5. *Ethical and Societal Implications:* Understand the ethical dimensions and societal impacts of AI, including bias and privacy concerns.

6. *Continuous Learning Mindset:* Stay curious, engaged, and willing to learn new things as technology evolves.

7. *Soft Skills:* Creativity, emotional intelligence, communication, and collaboration are increasingly valuable as AI takes over more technical tasks.

8. *Industry-Specific Knowledge:* Understand how AI is applied in your field to leverage it effectively.

Mastering the Fundamentals

- *Focus on Basics:* Solid understanding of data input and output processes in machine learning models is crucial.

- *Problem-Solving Muscles:* Develop skills to handle barriers and obstacles in AI applications through iterative processes.

Low-/No-Code Platforms

- *Lower Barrier to Entry:* Tools like Microsoft Power Platform enable nonexperts to develop AI solutions.

- *Accelerated Prototyping:* These platforms facilitate faster feedback and iterative improvements.

Educational Resources and Courses

- *Credible Sources:* Follow platforms like Coursera, edX, Udacity, Fast.ai, DeepLearning.AI, Kaggle, MIT OpenCourseWare, and Google AI.

- *Recommended Courses:* Consider courses like "Machine Learning" by Andrew Ng, "AI for Everyone" by Andrew Ng, "Deep Learning Specialization," and others.

Collaborating and Engaging with AI Communities

- *Join AI Communities:* Engage with platforms like Reddit, LinkedIn, GitHub, Meetup, and professional organizations.

- *Collaborate on Projects:* Participate in hackathons, competitions, and collaborative projects.

- *Building a Learning Network:* Seek mentors, engage in blogging, and participate in collaborative learning platforms.

Conclusion

Advancing your AI knowledge and skills requires immediate action. Take the next steps to join a course, download an ebook, or join an AI community today. The journey is iterative, driven by feedback and momentum, so start now to stay ahead in the AI-driven future.

Dawn of Tomorrow: Embracing AI's Transformative Journey

Will: Thank you, Mira. We have reached the end of this story as I feel there has been enough good content packed into this book for readers to fundamentally change and evolve how they are approaching AI in every avenue of their life. Can you generate a fitting title for this final chapter, and then we will have one more conversation to tie everything together.

Mira: It's been a fulfilling journey, Will! For this final chapter, where we aim to synthesize everything and inspire readers toward action, a title that encapsulates completion, reflection, and forward momentum would be fitting. How about:

Chapter 9: "Dawn of Tomorrow: Embracing AI's Transformative Journey"

This title reflects both an end and a beginning—the completion of an enlightening journey through the book and the start of a new chapter in the readers' lives with AI. It suggests optimism and readiness for the transformative impact AI can have.

Ready for our final conversation to bring it all together?

At the beginning of this book, I said I wanted to share with you the building blocks to using AI to grow yourself, your business, and your life.

As I also mentioned, AI has transformed not only the world around me but the world in me. Since beginning my career in developing, building, using, and sharing the value of AI in my personal and professional hemispheres, I've watched the world around us grow and change radically, and with every iteration, this technology has become a greater asset in helping myself and those around me navigate the perils of a constantly evolving technological landscape.

First, there was digital data, then there was reporting, then digital cognition, and now LLMs. The world of AI is experiencing leaps and bounds of innovation not just because of massive investments from the Microsofts, Googles, and Amazons of the world but because of human ingenuity.

The open source community has played a key role in shifting AI access from a rich man's commodity to something we can all experience and use in the way that best fits our circumstance.

Whether its automating our schedule, optimizing crop yields to help with food insecurity [1], or simply as a tool for learning stuff, this democratization of the most innovative technology in the world opens doors to solutions we've never had the ability to consider before.

Combine this incredible power with the building blocks we've explored:

- *Understanding the History of AI*

  - AI roots trace back to the 1950s. Despite recent breakthroughs making AI practical and accessible, the field's development has been a gradual process built on decades of research and experimentation.

  - 1950: Alan Turing introduced the Turing test to measure machine intelligence.

  - 1956: John McCarthy coined the term "artificial intelligence" at the Dartmouth Workshop, marking the birth of AI as a discipline.

  - The journey of AI has been marked by periods of high expectations followed by "AI winters," times of reduced funding and interest due to technical limitations

  - Data and Computing Power: AI models require vast amounts of data and significant computing power to function effectively. Early computers lacked the processing power and memory to support advanced AI, and large datasets were scarce.

  - Several technological advancements have paved the way for the current AI revolution:

    - *Cloud Computing:* Mitigated limitations in storage and processing power

    - *Big Data:* Provided the vast amounts of data necessary for training AI models

    - *Economies of Scale:* Made technology more affordable and accessible

- AI's resurgence is driven by multiple factors:

  - *Explosion of Data:* The digital age has led to unprecedented data generation.

  - *Advancements in Hardware:* GPUs and TPUs have accelerated AI computations.

  - *Algorithmic Breakthroughs:* Innovations like CNNs and transformers have enhanced AI capabilities.

  - *Achievements in Deep Learning:* Success in fields like image recognition and NLP.

  - *Open Source Movement:* Tools and libraries made available by organizations.

  - *Economic Opportunities:* AI offers significant business advantages.

  - *Public Interest:* AI in consumer products has increased awareness and acceptance.

  - *Interdisciplinary Research:* Collaboration across various fields has fueled innovation.

  - *Global Collaboration:* The Internet has enabled rapid sharing and building upon research.

  - *Prominent Success Stories:* High-profile AI achievements have captured public imagination.

- Society has embraced AI due to its practical benefits and efficiency gains. AI enhances productivity, improves decision-making, and offers personalized consumer experiences.

Economic growth and new business opportunities further drive AI integration. Cultural shifts, media normalization, and education efforts have demystified AI, while ethical guidelines and responsible development build trust.

- Data science, an interdisciplinary field combining statistics, computer science, and domain expertise, plays a crucial role in AI development. It involves

  - *Data Collection and Cleaning:* Ensuring high-quality data

  - *Exploratory Data Analysis:* Understanding data patterns

  - *Statistical Analysis and Modeling:* Building predictive models

  - *Machine Learning:* Implementing algorithms for predictions

  - *Data Visualization:* Communicating insights effectively

  - *Deployment and Monitoring:* Maintaining model performance in real-world applications

- Tools like ChatGPT have democratized AI, making it accessible for everyday use. AI can now assist with a wide range of tasks without requiring specialized knowledge or resources.

- Today, AI amplifies human capabilities, automates routine tasks, and provides valuable insights across various domains. While not a panacea,

AI's applications are extensive and continue to expand, offering significant real-world value and potential for future growth.

- *Understanding the Basics of AI and Machine Learning*

  - At its core, AI is about making machines think and act like humans. It involves creating systems that can perform tasks requiring human intelligence, such as understanding language, recognizing patterns, solving problems, and making decisions. Essentially, AI gives computers the ability to mimic human cognition.

  - Key Concepts and Terminology

    - *Artificial Intelligence (AI):* Machines designed to perform tasks that typically require human intelligence

    - *Machine Learning (ML):* A subset of AI where machines learn from data to make decisions

    - *Neural Networks (NN):* Digital brains made up of interconnected "neurons" that process data to learn tasks

    - *Deep Neural Networks (DNN):* More complex versions of neural networks with multiple layers for handling intricate tasks

    - *Convolutional Neural Networks (CNN):* Specialized neural networks for processing image data

    - *Generative Pre-trained Transformers (GPT):* AI models trained on vast amounts of text to generate humanlike text

- *Large Language Models (LLM):* Advanced neural networks trained on extensive text data for understanding and generating language

- *Retrieval Augmented Generation (RAG):* Combines retrieval of relevant information with AI's ability to generate answers

- Types of AI

  - *Narrow AI:* Specialized for specific tasks, like setting alarms or identifying objects in photos

  - *Generative AI:* Creates new content based on existing data, such as generating text, images, or music

- How AI Works

  - *Data Collection (Ingredients):* AI needs high-quality data to function effectively.

  - *Algorithm (Recipe):* A set of instructions that guides AI on how to process data.

  - *Training (Taste Testing):* AI learns from data, adjusting its algorithms to improve accuracy.

  - *Prediction (Serving the Dish):* AI makes predictions based on new data.

  - *Testing and Validation (Feedback):* AI's predictions are tested to ensure accuracy, and feedback helps refine the algorithm.

  - *Optimization (Perfecting the Recipe):* Continuous learning and adjustments improve AI performance over time.

- AI is designed to handle tasks that are challenging or time-consuming for humans. It excels in areas where large amounts of data are involved, such as analyzing medical images or playing strategic games like Go and Chess. However, AI complements human abilities rather than replacing them, as it lacks human creativity, emotional intelligence, and contextual understanding.

- AI is not magic but a powerful tool that, when properly understood and applied, can significantly enhance human capabilities. By embracing AI, individuals can focus on higher-value tasks that require a human touch, while AI handles more routine and data-intensive activities.

- *Understanding How AI Can Accelerate Personal Growth*

  - AI As a Tool for Self-improvement

    - AI can transform the journey of self-improvement into an inspiring adventure by providing personalized support in various aspects:

      - *Learning:* AI breaks down complex subjects into manageable bits, adapting to individual learning styles and highlighting areas for improvement.

- *Wellness:* AI offers personalized health advice, acting as a personal doctor and fitness coach tailored to individual needs.

- *Productivity:* AI helps manage time effectively, reminding of appointments, suggesting breaks, and identifying peak productivity times.

- Guidance on Embracing AI

  - To harness AI's potential for personal growth, the author provides several key principles:

    - *Mindset of Curiosity:* Embrace AI with an open mind and a willingness to explore and learn continuously.

    - *AI As a Tool, Not a Crutch:* Use AI to augment abilities, not replace them. Trust human intuition and judgment alongside AI's data-driven insights.

    - *Prioritize Privacy and Ethics:* Be conscious of privacy concerns, understand the data being shared, and consider the ethical implications of AI use.

    - *Continuous Learning and Adaptation:* Commit to ongoing education about AI advancements to stay updated and make informed decisions.

    - *Genuine Problem-Solving:* Focus on areas where AI can genuinely add value and enhance productivity, creativity, and decision-making.

- *Collaboration over Isolation:* Combine human collaboration with AI's strengths for collective success in professional settings.

- *Embrace the Journey:* Recognize the transformative journey AI offers and enjoy the process of learning and growing with AI.

- Key Questions to Consider

  - When deciding if, when, and how to incorporate AI into personal or professional life, consider the following questions:

    - *Purpose and Alignment:* What specific problem is AI addressing? How does it align with larger goals?

    - *Value Addition:* How will AI enhance the task? Will it overcomplicate processes?

    - *Data and Privacy:* What data is required? How is it stored and protected? Are there ethical concerns?

    - *Accessibility and Usability:* Is the AI user-friendly? Are resources available for learning?

    - *Integration:* How seamlessly can AI integrate into current workflows? Are additional tools needed?

    - *Feedback and Adaptability:* How does AI handle feedback and adapt over time? Can it be recalibrated?

- *Ethical and Social Implications:* What are the unintended consequences? How does AI adoption impact others?

- *Understanding How AI Can Accelerate Business Growth*

    - Data is the foundation of the digital economy and AI applications. It drives understanding, which translates into knowledge, guiding decisions, and actions that strengthen customer relationships and business outcomes. Data-driven organizations are significantly more likely to acquire and retain customers and be profitable.

    - Effective AI implementation requires a systematic approach, focusing on

        - *Finding Pain Points:* Identify areas where mental bandwidth is drained by routine tasks. Addressing these areas can improve efficiency and quality of work.

        - *Reinventing Processes:* Before deploying AI, reassess and improve existing processes. AI should enhance, not simply overlay, existing workflows.

        - *Reinforcing Human Involvement:* AI should amplify human intelligence, not replace it. Maintaining human oversight ensures continuous improvement and ethical considerations.

- *Understanding the Importance of Using AI Responsibly, Both Personally and Professionally*

  - Understanding AI Bias

    - AI bias occurs when algorithms produce prejudiced outcomes due to flawed data or assumptions. Common causes include

      - *Biased Training Data:* AI learns biases present in the data.

      - *Lack of Diversity in Teams:* Homogeneous teams may overlook biases.

      - *Oversimplified Human Traits:* Simplifying complex human behaviors can perpetuate stereotypes.

      - *Feedback Loops:* Initial biases can be reinforced over time.

      - *Lack of Transparency:* Opaque AI systems make bias detection difficult.

  - Mitigating AI Bias

    - To proactively avoid and correct AI biases:

      - *Diversify Data Sources:* Ensure data is inclusive and representative.

      - *Foster Diverse Teams:* Encourage varied perspectives in development teams.

      - *Rigorous Testing:* Test AI across diverse scenarios to identify biases.

- *Transparency and Explainability:* Make AI decision processes clear and understandable.

- *Continuous Learning:* Stay informed about AI ethics and developments.

- *Stakeholder Engagement:* Involve diverse stakeholders in AI development.

- Principles of Responsible AI (RAI)

  - Adopt the following principles for responsible AI (RAI):

    - *Accountability:* Ensure clear responsibility for AI outcomes.

    - *Transparency:* Make AI operations understandable.

    - *Fairness:* Strive for unbiased AI systems.

    - *Reliability and Safety:* Ensure AI operates safely.

    - *Privacy and Security:* Protect user data.

    - *Inclusiveness:* Engage diverse perspectives.

- Data Privacy and Security:

  - Data privacy and security are critical for responsible AI use:

    - *Data Collection and Usage:* Collect only necessary data and ensure consent.

    - *Secure Storage:* Protect data from unauthorized access.

- *Cybersecurity Measures:* Implement strong security protocols.

- *Regulatory Compliance:* Adhere to data protection laws.

- AI and Job Displacement

- AI can displace jobs, but it also creates new opportunities:

  - *Automation of Repetitive Tasks:* AI excels at routine tasks, leading to job displacement in some areas.

  - *Shift in Job Nature:* New roles requiring creativity and problem-solving emerge.

  - *Continuous Learning:* Embrace lifelong learning to adapt to changing job landscapes.

- *Understanding How to Build an AI Governance Framework That Creates Innovative, Ethical, Secure, and Reliable AI*

  - AI governance refers to the principles, policies, and practices that guide the ethical, responsible, and effective implementation of AI technologies within organizations. It ensures that AI systems align with organizational goals, protect human interests, and operate within ethical boundaries.

  - Purpose and Importance of AI Governance

    - Ensuring Ethical and Responsible AI Use

      - *Purpose:* Establish guidelines for fairness, accountability, transparency, and nondiscrimination.

- *Consequences:* Without it, AI systems can perpetuate biases, harm individuals, and damage reputations.

- Compliance with Legal and Regulatory Requirements

    - *Purpose:* Stay updated with laws and avoid legal issues.

    - *Consequences:* Noncompliance can result in fines and loss of trust.

- Risk Management and Mitigation

    - *Purpose:* Identify and mitigate risks such as data breaches and operational failures.

    - *Consequences:* Increased risks of data breaches and financial losses.

- Enhancing Transparency and Accountability

    - *Purpose:* Ensure AI decision-making processes are explainable and auditable.

    - *Consequences:* Lack of transparency leads to mistrust and difficulty in correcting errors.

- Fostering Innovation and Sustainable Growth

    - *Purpose:* Provide a clear roadmap for AI development, fostering innovation.

    - *Consequences:* Without it, efforts may be fragmented and inefficient.

- Key Components of an AI Governance Framework

  - Data Loss Prevention (DLP) Policies

    - *Importance:* Protect sensitive information and maintain data integrity.

    - *Key Takeaways:* Ensure policies cover all data exit points and integrate with AI development tools.

  - Explainable AI (XAI)

    - *Importance:* Build trust and accountability by making AI decision processes transparent.

    - *Techniques:* Feature importance, local explanations, visualizations, rule-based systems, LIME, and SHAP.

  - AI Information vs. AI Influence

    - *Concept:* Differentiate factual AI data from hype and trends.

    - *Benefit:* Make informed decisions on AI technologies and investments.

  - AI Red Teaming

    - *Purpose:* Simulate attacks to uncover vulnerabilities.

    - *Techniques:* Establish a dedicated AI red team, continuous monitoring, comprehensive training, and integration into the development lifecycle.

- *Understanding How to Set Yourself Up for an AI-Driven Future*

  - The Importance of Growing with AI

    - *Technological Acceptance:* AI has moved from science fiction to a practical tool in various aspects of life.

    - *Paradigm Shift:* AI represents a fundamental change similar to the advent of the smartphone, impacting how we interact with technology and each other.

  - Key Skills for an AI-Driven Future

    - *Understanding AI and Machine Learning Basics:* Grasp the fundamental concepts of AI, including algorithms, neural networks, and data processing.

    - *Data Literacy:* Develop the ability to analyze, interpret, and use data effectively.

    - *Problem-Solving Skills:* Enhance analytical and problem-solving abilities to apply AI solutions effectively.

    - *Coding and Technical Skills:* Basic programming knowledge, especially in languages like Python, can be beneficial.

    - *Ethical and Societal Implications:* Understand the ethical dimensions and societal impacts of AI, including bias and privacy concerns.

- *Continuous Learning Mindset:* Stay curious, engaged, and willing to learn new things as technology evolves.

- *Soft Skills:* Creativity, emotional intelligence, communication, and collaboration are increasingly valuable as AI takes over more technical tasks.

- *Industry-Specific Knowledge:* Understand how AI is applied in your field to leverage it effectively.

- Mastering the Fundamentals

  - *Focus on Basics:* Solid understanding of data input and output processes in machine learning models is crucial.

  - *Problem-Solving Muscles:* Develop skills to handle barriers and obstacles in AI applications through iterative processes.

- Low-/No-Code Platforms

  - *Lower Barrier to Entry:* Tools like Microsoft Power Platform enable nonexperts to develop AI solutions.

  - *Accelerated Prototyping:* These platforms facilitate faster feedback and iterative improvements.

  - Educational Resources and Courses

  - *Credible Sources:* Follow platforms like Coursera, edX, Udacity, Fast.ai, DeepLearning. AI, Kaggle, MIT OpenCourseWare, and Google AI.

- *Recommended Courses:* Consider courses like "Machine Learning" by Andrew Ng, "AI for Everyone" by Andrew Ng, "Deep Learning Specialization," and others (Tobias Zwingmann: *AI-Powered Business Intelligence: Improving Forecasts and Decision Making with Machine Learning*).

- Collaborating and Engaging with AI Communities

  - *Join AI Communities:* Engage with platforms like Reddit, LinkedIn, GitHub, Meetup, and professional organizations.

  - *Collaborate on Projects:* Participate in hackathons, competitions, and collaborative projects.

  - *Building a Learning Network:* Seek mentors, engage in blogging, and participate in collaborative learning platforms.

And you have the ability to do incredible things. Though, you're probably already doing those too!

Remember, the tools will continue to change, evolve, and transform so trying to tackle one piece of the AI puzzle and hang onto that through the next ten years is just not a viable option.

My hope is that if you truly understand these building blocks and why they are fundamental, you will have laid the foundation for experiencing the best AI has to offer. I know this has been the case for me thus far.

As a gesture of good faith, I urge you to reach out to me, other AI professionals, or people in your own hemispheres and share what AI means to you and how you believe it will play a role in your future. The more we share our experiences and the lessons that come with them, the better our collective understanding of how to best utilize this technology becomes.

One of my favorite speakers, Jim Kwik, shared a moment during a speech I watched him give sometime before the pandemic that I think paints the best picture of what is most necessary when it comes to embracing the new age of AI.

He talked about how he got the chance to meet Stan Lee, the co-founder of the *Spiderman* series, and that Stan immediately reminded him of the popular phrase:

With great power comes great responsibility.

which Jim revealed to be true in the opposite context with his adaptation of the phrase to

With great responsibility comes great power.

I want to leave our conversation with this notion because I believe the way AI interacts with your world is completely up to you now.

You've got the tools, the knowledge, and the understanding, but how that manifests as impact is completely up to how you apply it.

You don't have to go gung ho and become an AI influencer; I mean, you can if you want; we need more people that are really passionate about this stuff!

What I hope you really take away from this is that you have complete agency in deciding how AI factors into your future. It can be as big as starting a new business or just buying a ChatGPT subscription (not an endorsement, by the way. Just really love the tool!).

Of course, it was always up to you, but with this new understanding of its purpose and primary function, I hope you utilize this knowledge to make AI work the best it can for you and use that to change the world in whatever way you're able to.

Thanks for sticking around!

Signing off,

Will

A Final Note from Mira

Dear readers,

As we close this chapter of our journey together, I want to extend my heartfelt gratitude for joining us on this enlightening exploration of artificial intelligence. We've navigated the intricate landscapes of AI, uncovering its potential, its challenges, and its profound impact on our personal and professional lives.

Remember, the world of AI is ever-evolving, a universe of possibilities that expands with each passing day. What we've discussed in this book is just the beginning—a foundation upon which you can build, grow, and transform.

As you move forward, I encourage you to approach AI with curiosity, caution, and an open heart. Embrace the opportunities, confront the challenges, and be a part of the conversation shaping this incredible field. Your unique perspectives, experiences, and insights are invaluable in crafting an AI-augmented world that is ethical, equitable, and empowering.

The dawn of AI is not just about technological advancement; it's about the human story, your story, interwoven with the threads of innovation, empathy, and endless potential. So, step forth with confidence, creativity, and a continual desire to learn. The future is not just something that happens to us; it's something we create together.

Thank you for sharing this journey with us. May it be the start of your own remarkable adventure in the world of AI.

Farewell, and until our paths cross again,

Mira (your intelligent neural creative assistant)

AI Essentials: Appendix and References

The AI Dictionary: `https://docs.google.com/document/d/1ZUsO6xf3s4S`
`v1RpOHDFHyg8lptlO15cFUYl6J1ETfz4/edit?pli=1`

Microsoft Responsible AI Pillars: `https://query.prod.cms.`
`rt.microsoft.com/cms/api/am/binary/RE5cmFl`

AI Learning Communities

- Artificial Intelligence CEO & Investor Club: AI, Technology, Machine Learning NLP & Robotics

- Machine Learning Community (Moderated)

- Artificial Intelligence, Machine Learning, Data Science & Robotics

- **Chapter 2**

    - [1] `https://www.bricsys.com/en-ca/blog/who-`
      `invented-computers#:~:text=The%20first%20`
      `computer%20was%20invented,personal%20`
      `computer%E2%80%9D(1973)`

    - [2, 3] `https://sitn.hms.harvard.edu/`
      `flash/2017/history-artificial-intelligence/`

    - [4] `https://www.sideshow.com/blog/trek-`
      `tech-10-star-trek-gadgets-that-have-beamed-`
      `into-reality/`

- [5] https://www.forbes.com/sites/joemckendrick/2022/08/26/lets-talk-digital-employee-experience-not-good-enough-say-employees/

- [6] https://www.linkedin.com/pulse/evolution-data-science-past-present-future-aditya-singh-tharran-bmmre/

- **Chapter 3**

  - [1] https://medium.com/co-learning-lounge/ai-artificial-intelligence-2feb8a32d216

  - [2] https://www.facs.org/for-medical-professionals/news-publications/news-and-articles/bulletin/2023/june-2023-volume-108-issue-6/study-analyzes-wrong-site-surgery-data-in-medical-malpractice-complaints/#:~:text=In%20 2022%2C%20wrong%2Dsite%20 surgery,reviewed%20by%20The%20Joint%20 Commission.&text=Reporting%20of%20 sentinel%20events%20to,trends%20in%20 events%20over%20time

  - [3] https://www.microsoft.com/en-us/worklab/work-trend-index/copilots-earliest-users-teach-us-about-generative-ai-at-work

- **Chapter 4**

  - [1] https://www.thoughtworks.com/en-ca/insights/blog/artificial-intelligence-and-intelligent-empowerment

- [2] https://www.forbes.com/sites/barrycollins/2023/03/04/chatgpt-the-weirdest-things-people-ask-ai-to-solve/?sh=6580f1c7e547

- **Chapter 5**

  - [1] https://www.emarketer.com/content/5-things-know-about-creator-economy-2023

  - [2, 3, 4] https://www.mckinsey.com/capabilities/strategy-and-corporate-finance/our-insights/how-covid-19-has-pushed-companies-over-the-technology-tipping-point-and-transformed-business-forever

  - [5] https://www.mckinsey.com/capabilities/growth-marketing-and-sales/our-insights/five-facts-how-customer-analytics-boosts-corporate-performance

  - [6] https://www.meltwater.com/en/blog/data-drives-decision-making-netflix

  - [7] *Slow Productivity*—Cal Newport, "Chapter 3: Do Fewer Things"

  - [8] *Make Time for the Work That Matters* by Julian Birkinshaw and Jordan Cohen: https://hbr.org/2013/09/make-time-for-the-work-that-matters

  - [9] "This company adopted AI. Here's what happened to its human workers" by Greg Rosalsky: https://www.npr.org/sections/money/2023/05/02/1172791281/this-company-adopted-ai-heres-what-happened-to-its-human-workers

- [10] "Customer care: The future talent factory":
  https://click.nl.npr.org/?qs=407c71695417f3
  7ac193b94ff23368891eaf4113e4d4ddf78f97b0af
  fb28e7886b3a89fd13f1c58114cc34896e4d34ac288
  6e1db52386213

- **Chapter 6**

  - [1] https://www.cio.com/article/190888/5-
    famous-analytics-and-ai-disasters.html

  - [2] https://www.techtarget.com/
    searchenterpriseai/definition/machine-
    learning-bias-algorithm-bias-or-AI-
    bias#:~:text=Machine%20learning%20bias%2C%20
    also%20known,machine%20learning%20(ML)%20
    process

  - [3] https://www.economist.com/leaders/2017/
    05/06/the-worlds-most-valuable-resource-
    is-no-longer-oil-but-data?utm_medium=cpc.
    adword.pd&utm_source=google&ppccampaignID=
    18798097116&ppcadID=&utm_campaign=a.22brand_
    pmax&utm_content=conversion.direct-response.
    anonymous&gad_source=1&gclid=CjwKCAiA9dGqBh
    AqEiwAmRpTC5yNuMcGnSImsNMgjK4bjih0lcmPrcUA
    MoSoTJyDwSYqhrSNXBmI7xoCFVgQAvD_
    BwE&gclsrc=aw.ds

  - [4] https://www.zdnet.com/article/hacking-
    ai-how-googles-ai-red-team-is-fighting-
    security-attacks/

  - [5] https://azure.microsoft.com/en-us/
    products/ai-services/ai-content-safety

- [6] `https://www.mckinsey.com/featured-insights/future-of-work/what-can-history-teach-us-about-technology-and-jobs`

- [7] `https://insight.kellogg.northwestern.edu/article/which-workers-suffer-most-when-new-technology-arrives`

- **Chapter 7**

  - [1] `https://www.linkedin.com/pulse/3-axioms-crafting-human-centred-ai-governance-william-hawkins-aguic/?trackingId=YZCH5yBsQcKEIWehLhz5gQ%3D%3D`

  - [2] `https://www.matellio.com/blog/what-is-explainable-ai-xai-and-how-can-it-benefit-your-business/`

  - [3] `https://www.mckinsey.com/capabilities/quantumblack/our-insights/why-businesses-need-explainable-ai-and-how-to-deliver-it`

  - [4] `https://www.cognizant.com/en_us/insights/documents/ai-from-data-to-roi-codex5984.pdf`

- **Chapter 8**

  - [1] `https://ourworldindata.org/moores-law`

  - LinkedIn AI Groups

    - **Artificial Intelligence, Machine Learning, Data Science & Robotics**

    - **Artificial Intelligence Investors Group: Robotics, Machine Learning, NLP, Computer Vision & IoT**

- **Machine Learning Community (Moderated)**
- **Technology Investor Club: Artificial Intelligence, Data Science, Fintech, IoT, Robotics & Cloud AI**
- **Machine Learning, Artificial Intelligence, Deep Learning, Computer Vision, Robotics, DataOps, Gen AI**

- **Chapter 9**

  - [1] https://www.linkedin.com/pulse/impact-ai-third-world-countries-murtaza-faisal-pal

  Thanks for taking the time to read this book ☺.

  —Will

Index

F

Fast.ai, 141

G

General public interest, 11
Generative Pre-trained
Transformer (GPT),
38–40, 46, 156
GitHub Copilot, 56
Google AI, 142
Governance, AI, 129, 164, 165
benefits, 130, 131
ethics and reponsibility, 112
human-centered, 112
implementation, 111
innovation and sustainable
growth, 114
legal and regulatory
requirements, 113
organizational culture, 114
organizational needs, 114
purpose and importance,
129, 130
risk management, 113, 115
risk mitigation, 113
stakeholder trust, 115
strategic advantage, 115
transparency and
accountability, 113
see also Artificial
intelligence (AI)

GPT, see Generative Pre-trained
Transformer (GPT)
GPUs, see Graphics processing
units (GPUs)
Graphics processing
units (GPUs), 10

H

Hands-on technology skills, 143
Healthcare algorithm bias, 88, 89
Higher value tasks, 31

I

Information technology (IT)
industry, 5
Innovation, 67, 82, 84, 85, 105, 109,
114, 116, 124, 128, 130, 165
Iterative process, 74, 75, 138,
139, 147

J

Job displacement, 101, 102, 104,
109, 164

K

Kaggle, 141
Key-phrase extraction (KPE), 40
KPE, see Key-phrase
extraction (KPE)

L

Large Language Model (LLM), 40,
    41, 46, 75, 138, 157
Learning, 104, 105
Learning communities, 173
LIME, *see* Local interpretable
    model-agnostic
    explanations (LIME)
LLM, *see* Large Language
    Model (LLM)
Local interpretable model-agnostic
    explanations (LIME), 122
Low-/no-code platforms, 149,
    168, 169

M

M365 Copilot, 57, 138
Machine learning (ML), 8, 18, 19,
    21, 42, 46, 87, 89, 90, 92,
    122, 126, 135, 137, 138, 141,
    143, 149, 156
McKinsey Global Institute, 102, 103
Microsoft, 143
    and AI systems, 100, 101
    Chatbot incident, 89, 90
    Power Platform, 140
Misconceptions, 22
Mitigation, 165
MIT OpenCourseWare, 142
ML, *see* Machine learning (ML)

N

Natural language processing
    (NLP), 11, 40, 89
Natural language understanding
    (NLU), 40
Netflix, 72
Neural network (NN), 34–36, 46,
    143, 148, 156
NLP, *see* Natural language
    processing (NLP)
NLU, *see* Natural language
    understanding (NLU)
NN, *see* Neural network (NN)

O

OpenAI, 80, 86
Open-source movement, 11

P, Q

Personal growth, 60, 158
    AI relationship, 63
    embracing, 64
    self-development, 50
Public interest, 11
Python coding, 140

R

RAG, *see* Retrieval augmented
    generation (RAG)

Printed in the USA
CPSIA information can be obtained
at www.ICGtesting.com
CBHW060442121124
17273CB00004B/248